*THE CENTERS OF CIVILIZATION SERIES*

# ROME

*In the Augustan Age*

# ROME

## IN THE AUGUSTAN AGE

BY

Henry Thompson Rowell

NORMAN

*UNIVERSITY OF OKLAHOMA PRESS*

BY HENRY THOMPSON ROWELL

(Ed.) Jérôme Carcopino, *Daily Life in Ancient Rome*
(New Haven, 1940)
*Rome in the Augustan Age*
(Norman, 1962)

Library of Congress Catalog Card Number: 62-11277

Copyright 1962 by the University of Oklahoma Press, Publishing Division of the University. Composed and printed at Norman, Oklahoma, U.S.A., by the University of Oklahoma Press. First edition.

UXORI  CARISSIMAE

# PREFACE

WHEN THE University of Oklahoma Press invited me to write a book on Rome in the Age of Augustus for its Centers of Civilization Series, I accepted with gratitude and pleasure. It was a welcome opportunity to describe and interpret for the reader who did not already possess a specialized knowledge of the subject an important period in the life of a city which occupies a place of unique importance in the history of Western civilization. I was aware when I began my work of the vast quantity of material which I would have to read, if the book was to make any pretension to completeness, and of the complexity of many of the problems I would have to resolve. I did not fully realize, however, the number of laborious compromises which would have to be made and the painful difficulty of determining what to include and what to omit in order to remain within the number of pages at my disposal. Much was written which was later discarded, and much expanded beyond the original intention. This accounts in no small measure for the delays which have attended publication.

The completed book rather than its genesis is rightly, of course, the subject of the reader's interest. So that he may understand its character and know what to expect and not to expect in the text, a few words on certain methods of approach may be helpful.

First of all, an attempt has been made to set forth the facts as accurately as possible on the basis of the ancient evidence. When, as was often the case, the evidence was insufficient, faulty, obscure, or contradictory, the works of scholars who had made special studies of the problems involved were consulted. Among different interpretations and conclusions the one which seemed the best founded has been incorporated in the text, and the others have been passed over in silence. This procedure was imposed by the nature and length of the book. Nevertheless, as compensation for its shortcomings, uncertainty in important matters has usually been indicated.

As to the significance of the facts within whatever larger sphere or spheres they belong—historical, economic, religious—I have tried to formulate my own views. That they are often identical with views previously expressed by others will surprise no one who is at all familiar with the overwhelming mass of scholarship concerned with the Augustan Age. Many of them undoubtedly were absorbed and made my own in the course of years of reading. But I have not hesitated on occasion to go against the accepted trend when it seemed headed in a false direction.

It was not difficult to stay within the chronological limits of the Augustan Age in treating political, social, and ideological matters. Aspects of daily life, however, presented a problem. Our sources of knowledge in this area flow much more abundantly in later periods, and writers in this field have usually worked into a composite picture whatever pertinent information they could find, regardless of chronological considerations. In this book I have tried to avoid introducing material from other periods of the Empire. The picture is less complete for it, but it is more Augustan.

Finally, the reader will miss detailed discussions of Augustan literature and art, two of the greatest glories of the Augustan Age. The omission of a chapter on art is readily explained. I did not feel that I knew enough about the development of art in Rome to place Augustan art in its proper artistic relationship to the whole and to decide with competence between the various views which have been expressed by experts about it. Moreover, there can be no fruitful examination of artistic techniques without a relatively large number of illustrations. On the other hand, I have described certain artistic monuments as reflections of the mental climate of the Augustan Age.

With regard to the literature, it did not seem possible to discuss it as literature without devoting to it an inordinately large part of the book. The reader can easily find elsewhere expositions of Augustan literature containing detailed discussions of the themes, forms, and influences which belong to the sphere of literary history and criticism. When I decided to accord the space which I could have devoted to the authors to such subjects as the nature of the population, the physical aspect of the city, and the games, I laid myself open to the charge of exchanging gold for a baser metal. But the baser metal was an integral part of the Augustan city which might not be as well known to the non-classicist. However, references have been made to Augustan writers on occasions when they struck a note which gave added force or clarity to a particular theme. I have also attempted in the first chapter to pay an inadequate but sincere tribute to Augustan literature and art.

The ancient sources have usually been paraphrased. But I have often let Augustus speak for himself in direct translation. The document in which his words are preserved is known as the *Res Gestae Divi Augusti* (Deeds of the Deified Augustus), generally cited as *Res Gestae*. It is an account which he personally composed of his administration and achievements and which was originally engraved on bronze tablets set up before his mausoleum at Rome. The original has been lost, but enough survives from copies on monuments in Asia Minor to make possible a virtually complete reconstruction. It is the single most important inscription which has come down to us from classical antiquity.

Another word may be said appropriately here about the sums of money which will be encountered in this book. They will be given in numbers of sesterces, the monetary unit which Augustus preferred to use in the *Res Gestae*. It is quite impossible to figure out the exact buying power of the Augustan sesterce, to say nothing of calculating its equivalent in modern monetary terms. In fact, it has been held that the historical investigation of the buying power of money corresponds in the economic field to the geometric problem of squaring the circle. Nevertheless, it has become traditional to equate the Roman sesterce with five American cents, regardless of the decline in buying power of sesterce and cent during their histories as common currency. For the sake of convenience, however, we shall adopt the equation, one sesterce = five cents, in the following pages, having reminded the reader that this is in truth a very rough approximation.

Finally, it was virtually impossible to write about the city of Rome in the Augustan Age without treating several aspects of the empire which Rome had created. The greatness of the Augustan constitution lay in the fact that it was successfully designed to give the Empire good government without removing Rome from her venerable position as the center and heart of the whole. The men who governed the provinces had served as city magistrates and been involved in city politics; the major policies and decisions which laid down the main lines of provincial administration were made by the Emperor in Rome with the advice and assistance of a city governmental body, the Roman Senate. Many of the major innovations which Augustus introduced into the political life of the city were caused by his solicitude for the Empire. There were, of course, local matters which Augustus chose to emphasize in the *Res Gestae*. But if we wish to understand the government of Augustan Rome in a large sense and the social structure which was part of it, we must attempt to see it as Augustus himself saw it—in imperial terms.

This, perhaps unfortunately, has meant a preponderance of constitutional and political history in the third chapter. The same can be said of Chapter II, "The Ascent to Power." Here the events have been reviewed to show the conditions under which the future emperor forged his career and the qualities which he possessed that enabled him to make these conditions into a path to power. At the same time this piece of background will explain much about the temper of the Roman people during the Augustan Age and the thoughts and feelings which the Emperor attempted to mold into an intellectual climate.

We shall begin with this part of Augustan history and carry it on in the third chapter to the new political order which was its result. We shall then look at the physical aspects of the city of Rome and, finally, at the world of religion, morals, and ideas.

The great debt incurred in writing even the most modest work on any aspect of classical antiquity is the debt to countless predecessors whose indefatigable work laid the foundations for any further reconstruction, be it in detail or synthesis. To all those whose scholarship I have used—and they are very many—I gladly acknowledge my indebtedness. I have discussed some of the matters appearing in this book with colleagues, but only casually. Consequently, the flaws as well as the virtues, if there are any, are entirely my own.

Two persons have shown a truly Vergilian patience while this book was being written: my wife, who spent many hours in typing, correcting, and improving the clarity of the text, and Mr. Savoie Lottinville, director of the University of Oklahoma Press, who affably never despaired, To both, my warmest thanks.

Henry Thompson Rowell

*Rome, Italy*
*January 2, 1962*

# Contents

## M A P

# ROME

*In the Augustan Age*

# I

# THE AUGUSTAN
# INHERITANCE

OF THE SEVERAL PERIODS OF TIME into which we conveniently divide the momentous history of the city of Rome, that in which we speak of Rome as ancient is by far the longest.

Archaeological evidence indicates that the earliest settlements on the Roman hills were made in the eighth century B.C., and it is clear that in time these settlements united to form a political entity which we can properly call a city. But how and when this took place is still a matter of controversy. For our immediate purpose, which is to furnish here a general idea of the length of Rome's ancient period, we can state that the history of Rome began in the eighth century B.C. when the first seeds were sown from which the historical city sprang.

The end of the period, although it lies under the clear light of history, is even more difficult to determine, if it can be determined at all. There was, of course, no given day, year, or decade when Rome ceased to be ancient and became medieval. Old and new elements existed side by side for considerable lengths of time, and both eliminations and fusions took place gradually. Moreover, certain fundamental changes, which at their completion make us feel that Rome has taken on a new complexion and character, did not begin or end simultaneously. In the evaluation of the relative importance of the shifting elements and patterns an unusually large part is played unavoidably by subjective judgment.

If we forego participation in the grand, and apparently endless, debate centered on the fall of Rome in the sense of the disintegration of the Roman Empire and its causes and look to the city proper for symptoms of change and transition which, taken together, might justify the view that they mark the end of an era, our eye is primarily attracted by the fifth century A.D. In the first place, Rome was captured and pillaged by barbarians three times: in 410, by Alaric and the Visigoths; in 455, by Genseric and the Vandals; and in 472, by Ricemer and Germanic mercenaries. Four years later another barbarian, Odoacer, deposed the last Roman emperor of the West, Romulus Augustulus, and proclaimed himself king. The year in which this political transformation occurred (476) has often been chosen as the last year of the Roman Empire in the West, although the fiction was maintained for some time that the Emperor of the East, whose court was at Constantinople, possessed the supreme authority under which Odoacer governed Italy as regent.

In the course of these barbarian occupations, the city does not seem to have suffered much serious physical damage—it was not put to the torch—apart from the loss of removable treasures, such as precious metals and works of art, which was particularly heavy under Genseric. Essential public works and buildings were repaired under the Gothic king Theodoric, who ruled Italy from 493 to 526, and the physical appearance of Rome continued to dazzle men's eyes in the fifth and sixth centuries. But the dazzling was caused by the city's accumulated architectural wealth, to

4

which the last imposing additions had been made at the end of the third and the beginning of the fourth centuries A.D. The city had exhausted its vitality in the great art of building, in which it had been pre-eminent. During the fourth century it maintained itself free of destruction by enemy violence, Christian fervor, private depredations, or sheer neglect. In the fifth century it began to be subject to all these ills.

Alaric did more than capture and pillage the city. He sounded a ghastly knell which was heard throughout the Empire by thoughtful men who could bring themselves to face the realities below the surface. For some eight hundred years before Alaric's blow, Rome had not been forcibly occupied by a foreign enemy. To be sure, the city had long ceased to be the political capital of the Empire, or of even the western half of it. Yet its prestige far surpassed that of any other city of the Mediterranean world, including the "Christian Rome," Constantinople, which Constantine had founded on the Bosporus. Rome's long and glorious history, her cultural traditions, and, above all, the role which she had played in founding, expanding, and consolidating the empire that bore her name had conspired to give her a position apart. It was natural, then, that there were those who refused to consider Rome's current misfortunes as anything more than passing adversities from which she would gather new strength. But Saint Jerome saw more clearly. After the city's fall to Alaric, he wrote in anguish from his monastery in Bethlehem, "in one city, the whole world has perished." Highly colored as the statement is by emotion, it contains more than a grain of prophetic truth. The learned Saint epitomized the feeling that many must have shared: a tragic event of universal importance had terminated an epoch with inexorable finality.

# ROME

The last half of the fourth century and the beginning of the fifth saw the last flowering of a Latin literature which was pagan in spirit and classical in form. Ammianus Marcellinus, the last of the noble line of the historians of antiquity, wrote his great history in Rome, and in Latin, although he was a Greek from Antioch by birth. The brilliant poetic talent of Claudius Claudianus was first displayed in Rome, and some of the finest passages in his poetry are devoted to eulogizing the city. Seven years after Alaric's departure, Rutilius Namatianus extolled the city's magnificence and the Empire's civilizing mission in verses of classical purity permeated with profound patriotic ardor. He predicted a rapid recovery from the late disaster. From the vantage point of history, his hymn to Rome is the city's swan song and the last great pagan poem of Roman classical literature in content, form, and spirit.

Finally, by the middle of the fifth century Rome had been largely Christianized. Imperial legislation concerned with pagan worship no longer vacillated between different degrees of repression and tolerance, as it did throughout most of the fourth century. The opposition to the rising tide of Christianity in Rome was centered in the pagan members of the senatorial aristocracy, who were striving to preserve the pagan culture with which they were imbued. They rallied around the great pagan writers of the past—Vergil in particular—in whom they saw not only perfect literary models for their own writings, but also repositories of information concerning all aspects of Rome in better days. This last stand of paganism in Rome, in which the literary past was made to serve both as a refuge from and a bulwark against the pressing realities of an ungracious present, was symptomatic of the romanticism which often characterizes the resistance to a changing culture.

The final triumph of Christianity in the fifth century A.D. was the successful termination of a spiritual revolution. In Rome it marked the end of a culture which had been firmly rooted in paganism. Christianity, of course, adopted and transformed much of the pagan material which it had inherited. The Christianized descendants of the pagan aristocracy would continue to be educated in the pagan classics, the older writers would still serve as models to be imitated in prose and poetry, and their achievements as artists would be sincerely admired. The first great Christian poet, Prudentius (last half of the fourth century and beginning of the fifth), was second to none in his veneration of Rome and her empire; he was also a master of the classical forms of Roman poetry. But he saw Rome blessed by divine dispensation in order that she might propagate the true faith, and his beautiful Horatian meters and reminiscences are consecrated to Christian rites, festivals, and martyrdoms. The fact is that a new world of beliefs and ideals had been created which could now develop itself freely. A new phenomenon, a universal church, had taken over the care and direction of men's souls. The city was well on the way to acquiring a new kind of importance: an importance that came from being the site of the graves of Saints Peter and Paul and the see of Peter's apostolic successor, the Bishop of Rome.

Spiritually, historically, and culturally, then, there is justification in holding that the ancient period of Rome's existence came to a close in the fifth century A.D., and if we will accept it as a terminal point, we can say that ancient Rome existed some twelve hundred years. Within this long period of time, the Augustan Age is conspicuous for its brevity. From the point of view of political history, it can be held that the Age began in 31 B.C., when the victory at Actium left Octavian, the later Emperor Augustus, the undisputed master of the Mediterranean world; or in 27, when the Republic was restored and the title of Augustus was bestowed upon the Emperor; or in 23, when Augustus received the tribunician power for life and began to reckon the years of his reign by the number of times he had held this power annually. The end of the Age is quite naturally made to coincide with the death in A.D. 14 of the man who gave it his name.

But cultural and artistic movements often do not accord with a chronology based on purely political considerations. They are known to develop before the historical events with which they will later be closely associated have taken place, and their own momentum will carry them on beyond the political period with which they have been identified. The two outstanding poets of the Augustan Age, Vergil and Horace, had already published works of considerable consequence before the battle of Actium: Vergil, the *Eclogues,* and Horace, the first book of the *Satires.* At the other end of the era, Ovid continued to write after the death of Augustus. Hence, in treating the Augustan Age from a cultural point of view, exact dates for beginning and end tend to be misleading. It should suffice to hold in mind that the ancient city of Rome reached its highest point of achievement in literature and the arts at the time when the Emperor Augustus possessed the concrete powers and moral authority which made him the most influential man in the Roman world. This is important in itself and explains at the same time why these few decades were chosen from the many centuries of Rome's existence in antiquity as the subject of this book.

The Age was culturally as well as politically Augustan. It is conceded that regardless of Rome's cultural eminence in the period, it would have taken its name from Augustus because of his supreme political power and the brilliant way in which he used it. But we do not have a situation here in which it is difficult, as it often is in other historical periods, to discern the relationship between an outburst of artistic productivity and the historical circumstances and political personalities under which and among whom it occurred. About the Augustan Age it can be stated categorically that the complex of cultural and intellectual phenomena which we call Augustan culture would never have come into being and assumed the forms which it actually assumed without the towering figure of the Emperor. The spirit of national revival, the veneration of the glories of the past, the return to the ways and virtues of ancestors—all vigorously fostered by Augustus—struck a responsive chord in men of genius. In few periods have the sovereign and the most consummate artists worked together more harmoniously toward a high moral and patriotic goal.

Augustus, of course, left his mark upon the entire Roman world, and his reorganization of the Empire, so radical that he may well be considered its founder, was his greatest and most enduring feat. But Rome, the seat of his empire, was the principal object of his care and affection. It was there that he built his most splendid monuments, formulated and executed his plans, and exercised the strongest influence on cultural matters. For our knowledge of the Augustan Age, we must go first to Rome.

Moreover, Rome in literature and art never seemed more Roman than in this Age of Augustus. A long road had been traveled since the beginnings of Latin literature when, to cite Horace, "captured Greece took captive its crude victor [the Roman] and introduced the arts into rustic Latium." Along this road which led from the Latin translation of

Homer's Odyssey by Livius Andronicus (last half of the third century B.C.), the work with which formal Latin literature began, to Horace himself and his Augustan contemporaries, the Roman genius had found opportunities to assert itself. Greek influence, of course, still made itself felt in the later period. But to a striking extent, the prose and poetry of the Age drew their strength, originality, and greatness from the social, intellectual, spiritual, and political environment in which they were created. Augustan literature is remarkably free of imitations of Greek models that float in a timeless limbo. Petronius showed fine discernment when two generations after Vergil's death he characterized the poet with the simple adjective "Roman." The quality which Petronius perceived is that which has won for certain odes of Horace the title "Roman Odes." At no time before or since was the best in the Roman character expressed with greater freshness, beauty, and conviction. No period in Rome's history seems to us to have been more thoroughly permeated by the Roman spirit in its loftiest and most patriotic vein.

This Roman quality is also manifest in many of the public monuments or works of art which owed their creation directly or indirectly to the Emperor. In them an idealized picture of Rome's past is often blended with dynastic propaganda and reminders of present blessings. The Roman had a strong feeling for records and traditions, for family and ancestors. In the noble families this feeling was inextricably entwined with the history of the state which family members had served and governed. The worthies of the past had shed luster not only on their descendants but also on the Roman family as a whole, the *gens Romana*. Augustus nurtured this pride on a national scale through architecture and the plastic arts.

This blending of past and present in the literature and art of the Augustan Age is not its least attractive or exciting feature. Just as in the realm of political history the Augustan constitution was composed of traditional elements so modified and rearranged that a new form of government was created, so in that of literature and art the old and familiar were made to acquire new values and a timely significance. The New Criticism has shown that fruitful results can be obtained from treating certain parts of Augustan literature as poetic entities endowed with a life of their own. This kind of critical aesthetic investigation has been unduly neglected in the past. But a full appreciation of this literature as a whole can never be attained except through an understanding of the historical climate in which it flourished.

The fact that the Augustan Age is acknowledged to be one of the classical periods par excellence in the whole of Greco-Roman antiquity deserves to be mentioned. Since the time when a classical author was defined in the first edition of the *Dictionary* of the French Academy (1694) as "a well-approved ancient author who commands authority in the material which he treats," there have been innumerable attempts to define the words "classic," "classical," and "classics," in the sense of "the classics." The word, of course, has never been restricted to Greco-Roman antiquity, and we can still speak of a modern work as "a classic." In doing so, we are returning to a meaning of the Latin *classicus,* which signified, when applied to a writer, that he was of the first class and worthy of being used as a model.

The acceptance of the ancient Greek and Latin authors, however, as the best literary models tended to give the word a specialized meaning and the phrase, "the classics," without further qualification, came to be understood as designating works of Greek and Roman literature. The concept of Greco-Roman antiquity as a period of uniform cultural excellence, a concept which prevailed in the eighteenth century, led to the creation of the phrase "classical antiquity." In this sense classical meant no more than Greco-Roman, and it was soon applied to almost anything which belonged to the Greco-Roman world. The Augustan Age is a part of classical antiquity, as we commonly use the phrase.

But the gradual realization that classical, that is Greco-Roman, antiquity contained many epochs with different levels of cultural achievement brought with it more realistic evaluations. The fundamental unity of the period as a whole within the history of mankind could not be overlooked or gainsaid. It was now necessary to define shorter periods within it, to distinguish their proper characteristics, and to assign them relative values. In the history of Greece the palm of excellence was awarded to the Age of Pericles. In the artistic vitality and genial perfection of its creations, only one other epoch in antiquity can be compared with it: the Age of Augustus in Rome. The two ages were quite different in many ways. But both were classical in the old sense of the word. In the midst of a cultural and historical environment which fertilized man's highest capabilities, men of genius, each in his way, produced works of so high a class that they have never been surpassed and have served as examples of the human spirit at its creative best for future generations.

# II

# THE ASCENT TO POWER

ON AUGUST 13, 14, and 15, of the year 29 B.C., Augustus, whom we shall call Octavian at this point of his career, celebrated three triumphs. In 33, he had successfully terminated a series of campaigns against the tribes of Dalmatia, which had been an initial step in extending the territory of the Empire to the Danube. On September 2, 31, his forces had decisively defeated those of Marcus Antonius and the Egyptian Queen Cleopatra at Actium. In the following year, he had captured Egypt. These were the occasions for the triumphs. At the moment, Octavian was finishing his thirty-fourth year and holding his fifth consulship. About three hundred thousand Roman soldiers had served under his command, and through them he finally established peace in the Roman world. To proclaim this achievement to the Roman people, the Temple of Janus had been closed in January by order of the Senate for the third time in Roman history. It was clear to everyone, including Octavian himself, that he was now the undisputed master of Rome and the Empire.

If he looked back upon his life at this time, he might well have marveled at the events that had brought him to this peak of glory and power. Much he could attribute to cool calculation, ruthlessness, persistence, and courage. He had known how to profit by the errors of his enemies, and, indeed, they had been many. But in certain circumstances, it must have seemed that Fortune was playing a very skillful game in his behalf.

First, there had been the second marriage of his father Gaius Octavius to Atia, the daughter of Marcus Atius and Julia, the sister of Gaius Julius Caesar. For his father this had been an excellent match. When he married Atia (c.65 B.C.), he had not progressed beyond the quaestorship, the lowest rung on the ladder of a senatorial career. This would not have been important, had he been a member of a distinguished family who could be expected to ascend, almost automatically, to a consulship. But this was not the case. Octavius was a "new man" and lacked "ancestors." This meant that he could not number among his forebears men who had occupied the higher magistracies, especially the consulship, which bestowed a title of political nobility on a family that was transmitted to its descendants. The ancestors of Octavius had been content to remain in the equestrian class, and he was the first of his family to enter upon a senatorial career. In it he did remarkably well, being praetor in 61 and governor of the province of Macedonia with the title of proconsul in the following year. There is little doubt that he would have been elected consul for 58, if death had not intervened.

But, more importantly, his marriage to Atia allied him with the eminent family of the Iulii Caesares, which enjoyed all the power and prestige which the Octavii lacked. Its members traced their lineage back to the goddess Venus through her son Aeneas, the founder of the Roman people, and his son Iulus, from whom the family name was derived. Less mythical ancestors had held high positions in the state, including the consulship. In the year of the marriage, Atia's uncle Gaius Julius Caesar was curule aedile and already an influential figure in Roman politics. It must have been obvious to the elder Octavius that he would make a very useful in-law.

The future Emperor Augustus was born to Octavius and Atia on September 23, 63 B.C., in Rome. He was given the name Gaius, which was traditional in the family, so that his full name was Gaius Octavius. After the death of his father (early in 59), his mother remarried, and he was brought up in the house of his stepfather, Lucius Marcius Philippus, who treated him with great affection. His education was carefully supervised, and he was given the opportunity of studying under some of the most famous teachers of the period. His training in rhetoric was directed by Epidius, in whose school he is said to have first met Vergil. His first public speech appears to have been delivered when he was only nine on the occasion of the funeral of his Aunt Julia, the only daughter of Julius Caesar. Julia's death had left Caesar without child or grandchild. His nearest male relatives by blood were the children and grandchildren of his two sisters. Without neglecting the descendants of his older sister, he reserved for Octavius, his grandnephew by his younger sister, a particular interest and sympathy. How far Caesar's discerning eye perceived potential greatness in Octavius is a matter of speculation. That Caesar was attracted by him and gave him opportunities to prove his abilities is a fact.

Because of his youth and ill health, Octavius was not able to participate in any of Caesar's campaigns, although he joined the Dictator in Spain after the battle of Munda (45 B.C.). He was allowed to play a part in the settlement of the province by serving as the advocate of peoples and individuals against whom charges had been preferred arising from the part they had played in the war. It was a test of the young man's loyalty, skill, and discretion, and he came

15

out of it with the esteem of Caesar and the gratitude of his clients. At Rome he had been elected to the college of priests in 47, through Caesar's influence, and had been put in charge of the Greek games that followed the dedication of the Temple of Venus the Mother (of the Julian family) in the following year.

Octavius was studying at Apollonia, in Epirus, across the Adriatic from the southern coast of Italy, when a messenger arrived from his mother with the tragic news that Caesar had been assassinated on the Ides of March (March 15, 44). His mother urged his immediate return to Rome. Friends at Apollonia advised him to join the army in Macedonia which was awaiting Caesar's arrival in order to march against Parthia; he would find it loyal to Caesar's memory and ready to return to Italy with him to exact vengeance for Caesar's death. Octavius realized that he could not act intelligently until he was better informed about affairs at home. He crossed quietly to Italy and there learned the details of Caesar's will.

The will was made on September 15, 45 B.C. In it, Caesar left two-thirds of his estate to Octavius and adopted him as his son. The exact nature of this testamentary adoption has been the subject of much debate. But what is important for us here is the way in which Octavius treated it. Having learned of it in Lupiae, a little town in the heel of Italy, he took the first momentous step on the path which would eventually lead him to supreme power. For he then decided that he would no longer be Octavius, the son of Octavius, but Caesar, the son of Caesar.

By adopting Caesar's name at once, even before the legal formalities were completed at Rome which would put him formally in possession of his inheritance, Octavius had proclaimed himself Caesar's son and heir and in one bold stroke

16

had created for himself a reservoir of power. He had made himself the person around whom all those who were loyal to Caesar's memory and incensed by his unworthy end could rally. Caesar's veterans had now found a new Caesar to whom they could transfer their devotion. Their allegiance had been pledged primarily to Caesar as their leader and general, not to the Senate and the Roman people. They had crossed the Rubicon with him in 49 B.C. and won victories for him against fellow Romans who had opposed with arms their general's ascent to supreme power. Caesar had died brutally murdered by men who had enjoyed his confidence and generosity. He now had a son to avenge the deed, and the magic name of Caesar was still alive.

On arriving in Rome early in May of 44, Octavius formally accepted his inheritance before the acting urban praetor, Gaius Antonius, brother of Marcus Antonius, who was then consul. Shortly thereafter he was permitted by another brother, Lucius, who was a tribune, to address the people. We can assume that he used this occasion to proclaim publicly that as son and heir he would undertake to pay Caesar's legacy to the Roman plebes—300 sesterces ($15.00) per man. To leave no possible doubt about the legitimacy of his testamentary adoption, Octavius wished to have it confirmed by a law passed in the curiate assembly, which was the usual procedure when a man was adopted who was not under his father's legal power (*patria potestas*). This move was frustrated by the Consul Antonius, who was beginning to see in Octavius a dangerous rival in the struggle for political power. This opposition made Octavius redouble his efforts to associate himself with Caesar's memory. At his own expense he held the games which Caesar had instituted in honor of his personal goddess of victory (*ludi Victoriae Caesaris,* July 20–30). During them a comet appeared which

17

was interpreted as a sign of Caesar's apotheosis. It hardly need be said that Octavius did nothing to discredit this interpretation.

As a matter of politics and honor, Caesar's legacy to the Roman plebs had to be paid as promptly as possible. Since there were at least 250,000 persons who were entitled to receive 300 sesterces each, the sum total amounted to 75,000,000 sesterces ($3,750,000) at the minimum. Then there were Caesar's veterans, who were impatiently waiting for bonuses in land or cash. The troops which had been assembled for Caesar's campaigns in the Orient and were still under arms had to be supplied and paid. Moreover, Octavius could certainly foresee what Cicero had foreseen in the middle of April: there would be more trouble with Marcus Antonius, who was acting as Caesar's political successor. Octavius needed to assure himself of the loyalty of Caesar's troops and to be able to outbid Antonius financially for their support.

An ancient tradition, hostile to Antonius and friendly to Octavius, would have us believe that the former seized and dissipated Caesar's private fortune as well as 700,000,-000 sesterces ($35,000,000) of public funds which had been earmarked for Caesar's impending campaigns and deposited in the temple of Ops on the Capitol, and that, consequently, Octavius was forced to sell Caesar's real properties at ruinous prices and to call on his coheirs and immediate relatives to sacrifice their financial interests so that he might meet his obligations.

The truth, however, seems to be that most of Caesar's private fortune in cash and the war appropriation had been transferred to Brundusium, on the Adriatic coast, which had been chosen as the principal base in Italy for the operations in the East. We know that Octavius, on his return to

Italy from Apollonia, hastened to Brundusium as soon as he had learned the terms of Caesar's will and decided to accept the inheritance with the obligations attached to it. There he was warmly greeted by the soldiers as Caesar's son and heir. As heir, Octavius had the right to take informal possession of Caesar's private funds; as private citizen, he could not legally touch a sesterce of the public appropriation. But the opportunity to secure strong financial sinews on which he could rely in a struggle for popularity and power could not be allowed to pass unexploited. A senatorial committee was later appointed to investigate the disappearance of the 700 millions of public funds. But it never acted, for the army that Octavius raised and supported with his money was then fighting against Antonius on the side of the Senate.

The formation of this army is the first thing to be mentioned in the *Res Gestae*: "At the age of nineteen I raised an army on my private initiative, and at my private expense, by means of which I liberated the state from the oppression of a tyrannical faction. On this account the Senate, in decrees which did me honor, took me into its order in the consulship of Gaius Pansa and Aulus Hirtius [43 B.C.], conferring upon me the right of speaking among the former consuls, and gave me the imperium. The Senate ordered me, as propraetor, in conjunction with the consuls to take care that the state should come to no harm. In the same year, when both consuls had fallen in war, the people elected me consul and one of a board of three men charged with settling public affairs."

These matter-of-fact sentences cover a period from the autumn of 44 to the establishment of the second triumvirate by the *lex Titia* on November 27 of the year 43. Within a little more than a year's time, the "boy," as he was referred to in a condescending way by Antonius, had risen from the status of a private citizen to the highest regular magistracy of the Roman state, the consulship, and beyond that to an irregular, though legal, position of supreme power which he shared with Marcus Antonius and Aemilius Lepidus. This remarkable ascent on the part of a man who had not yet reached his twenty-first birthday could not, of course, have been carried out without military strength. But the manner in which this strength was acquired and used was a masterpiece of cold and effective calculation.

In October, Octavius began to recruit his private army from among Caesar's veterans in Campania, south of Rome. By the beginning of November, he had collected three thousand men. At the time a large part of the Senate had become thoroughly disgusted with the capricious and tyrannical behavior of Antonius. Antonius had turned the city into an armed camp and had even stated in a burst of anger that he would illegally remain in Rome with his army after his consulship had terminated (on December 31, 44). Before his military strength and violence the Senate was helpless. Antonius was still consul and by virtue of his office was the legitimate commander of all troops in Italy. The other consul, Publius Dolabella, had already set out, or was about to set out, for the province of Syria, the governorship of which he owed to his colleague's favor. No resistance to Antonius could be expected from this quarter. Apparently, the republicans in the Senate, that is, the members who had hoped that the removal of Caesar would automatically restore the body to its old authority, would have to wait until January 1, 43, to take any effective action. On that date two new consuls, Aulus Hirtius and Gaius Pansa, would enter office. They not only possessed the right to raise

20

troops but, it was thought, would duly respect the wishes of the Senate.

To assure himself a position of strength in Italy, Antonius had had the people assign to him the governorship of the province of Cisalpine Gaul (roughly the Po Valley) for a period of five years, beginning in 43. It was then being governed by Decimus Brutus, one of Caesar's murderers. Antonius also recalled four of the legions from Macedonia which were waiting to take part in Caesar's campaigns in the East at the time of his death. Antonius left Rome on October 9 to take command of them at Brundusium.

At the beginning of November, while Antonius was still absent from Rome, Octavius wrote to Cicero seeking his advice. Cicero had not participated in the conspiracy against Caesar, although he had approved its result. He was the most influential man among the republicans and a bitter enemy of Antonius. Octavius asked him whether he should march on Rome with his veterans, attempt to intercept Antonius, who was returning to the city with one legion, or set out to meet the three Macedonian legions which were making their way up the Adriatic coast in the hope that they could transfer their allegiance from Antonius to himself. Cicero advised him to go to Rome, where he would find the common people and also men of substance on his side if he could make them believe in his loyalty. Octavius followed Cicero's advice, but could not persuade him to come to Rome himself from his villa at Puteoli. Cicero did not have confidence in Octavius' experience and intentions.

In Rome, Octavius put himself and his army at the disposal of the Senate against Antonius, whom he attacked bitterly in a public speech. Antonius now realized fully that Octavius was his most serious rival and was endeavoring to

21

frustrate and humiliate him at every turn. Octavius' offer to support the Senate must have been sweet music to the ears of the defenseless republicans. But there was a loud discordant note in an oath in which Octavius revealed his intention of attaining his father's honors. The impending battle for the control of the city was never fought. A number of Octavius' soldiers were also devoted to Antonius and refused to fight against him. He allowed them to depart and soon found himself in no position to meet his rival in the field. Octavius withdrew to Arretium (Arezzo) to repair his forces, and Antonius entered Rome unmolested.

Political necessity thus began to make strange bedfellows of the man who proclaimed himself Caesar's son and heir and the men who had rejoiced at Caesar's murder. The Senate needed military strength to combat Antonius, and Octavius had made his army available. But if it was to be used in behalf of the Senate and under the Senate's guidance, Octavius' position as commander had to be legalized and his soldiers made responsible to the Roman state. No one but the Senate or the Roman people could confer upon Octavius the official magistracy with the imperium which would give him the legal right to command his troops. Octavius perceived that the real struggle which lay directly ahead of him was with Antonius, a consul and soon to be a former-consul, to whom many of Caesar's soldiers were still loyal. He needed a position within the regular structure of the government and the respectability which senatorial rank would give him. He also needed the additional strength which the fresh troops certain to be raised by the consuls of 43 to fight Antonius would bring to his side. He can have had no illusions that the Senate cherished him for his own sake. It was being compelled to turn to him by military necessity. Whatever alliance he made with it would not last indefinitely. But it would last until Antonius was defeated, and, in the meantime, he would be able to consolidate his power in a legitimate manner.

There were, of course, many misgivings on the part of the republicans. Cicero, in particular, found difficulty in making up his mind about the trustworthiness of his new young friend. But Octavius soon gave a convincing demonstration of his usefulness.

On November 28, the news reached Rome that he had persuaded two of the Macedonian legions to defect from Antonius and come over to him. He now had a first-class fighting force, and, rather than be caught in Rome by it, Antonius hastily abandoned the city and traveled northward to Cisalpine Gaul, which was to become his province on January 1. For the first time in many months, the Senate could breathe freely. Octavius had made this possible.

By December 20, even Cicero's doubts had been assuaged. On that day he delivered a speech before the Senate (the third *Philippic*) in which he warmly praised Octavius and his army as defenders of the state and moved that the new consuls, on taking office, should bring before the Senate the matter of rewarding them appropriately. This was done in a session on January 1, 43, in which Cicero moved that Octavius should be declared a senator with the rank of propraetor and the right of voting among those who had already held the regular praetorship and, furthermore, that in regard to any magistracy for which he might stand in the future, he should be considered to have held the quaestorship in 44. In its action, the Senate went even further. It decreed that Octavius should vote among the former-consuls and ordered him in conjunction with the new consuls to make war on Antonius. It matters little how many senators voted for these measures in the tacit belief that the "boy" should be praised, honored, and dismissed after he had served their purpose. On January 7, Octavius assumed the fasces which symbolized the fact that he now commanded his army as a Roman magistrate.

Decimus Brutus had refused to hand over the province of Cisalpine Gaul to Antonius when he arrived there in December. In so doing he was within his rights. But on January 1 the province came to Antonius by law, and still Decimus continued to defy him. Antonius lay siege to the city of Mutina (Modena) where Decimus had taken refuge behind its walls. The first military task of Hirtius and Pansa, the new consuls, with the help of Octavius, would be to come to Decimus' rescue.

Octavius and his army were the first to enter Cisalpine Gaul. He did not attack Antonius, but pitched his camp at some distance from Bononia (Bologna), which Antonius had made his base of operations. Early in February, reinforcements arrived under Hirtius. The latter skirmished with Antonius, but there was no concerted attack. The arrival of the consul placed Octavius in a subordinate position which he appears to have accepted with good grace. In Rome too, the pace had slackened. Over Cicero's stubborn opposition, negotiations with Antonius were being carried out in the hope of avoiding civil war, and some of the governors of the western provinces who possessed armies were urging peaceful solution. But finally the other consul, Pansa, left Rome (about March 20) with an army of four newly recruited legions, and fighting began in earnest on April 15.

Octavius' feelings must have been mixed at this time. A victory by Antonius would mean an end to his own political career, if not to his very life. Moreover, it was only through a defeat which Octavius had taken part in inflicting that Antonius could be brought to consider him as an equal. But even a defeated Antonius, if he were still alive, would be a man to reckon with because of his military ability and the loyalty which he commanded among Caesar's former generals and many of their soldiers. Once Antonius was defeated, the Senate would undoubtedly show its true feelings toward Octavius and hasten to relegate him to obscurity. Then he would need the most powerful ally he could find, but one also with whom he could side on equal terms. Obviously, the man would be Antonius. Finally Octavius could not relish the thought that the chief purpose of the operation in which he was engaged was to rescue a man, Decimus Brutus, who had been one of the leading conspirators against his father's life. He had not forgotten his vow to take vengeance on his father's murderers. But he would have to bide his time.

There is no indication that Octavius did not carry out loyally the assignments given to him by his consular superiors during the fighting that went on between April 14 and April 21, when Antonius was finally defeated under the walls of Mutina, but escaped with his life and the remains of his six legions. In this battle Hirtius died. On the following day Pansa perished from wounds which he had received in an earlier engagement. In the course of the action, Octavius was acclaimed imperator by his troops.

When the news of the victory at Mutina reached Rome (about April 25), the Senate began to show its true sentiments toward Caesar's heir. After declaring Antonius a public enemy, it heaped honors on Decimus Brutus. The credit for the defeat of Antonius was attributed to him, although his role had been largely one of resistance within the walls of Mutina, and the honor of a triumph was conferred upon him. He was also given command of all the units of the consular armies which had survived and was instructed to pursue Antonius. The sop thrown to Octavius was an "ovation," an honor far below a triumph in importance. The Senate also then began to support wholeheartedly Marcus Brutus and Gaius Cassius, the prime movers of the conspiracy against Caesar, in their attempts to establish a strong military position in the eastern provinces. The Senate was again openly anti-Caesarian, and the process of dismissing the "boy" had begun.

The "boy," however, would not be dismissed. He rejected the request of Decimus for some of his legions and allowed Antonius and his lieutenant, Ventidius, to escape across the Maritime Alps into the province of Gallia Narbonensis (roughly the Provence of modern France), which was governed by Lepidus. In spite of the latter's frequent protestations of loyalty to the Senate, he was far more closely bound to Antonius. Both had served under Caesar, and at Caesar's death Antonius had had Lepidus elected pontifex maximus in Caesar's place, thus bestowing upon him the highest priesthood in the Roman state. Lepidus informed the Senate officially that at the approach of Antonius his soldiers refused to fight and intimated that he was compelled to join forces with Antonius. It can be doubted that much compulsion was needed.

The new army formed on May 29 consisted of ten full legions and the remains of the six which Antonius had commanded at Mutina. It was nominally commanded by Lepidus, but Antonius, who far surpassed him in ability, energy, and determination, was actually at its head. He realized that it would only be a matter of time before the other governors of western provinces, Munatius Plancus in northern Gaul and Asinius Pollio in farther Spain, both old Caesarians, would join him with their legions. Decimus Brutus had raised a new army and followed Antonius into

Gaul, but did not dare to engage the superior army of Antonius and Lepidus.

Octavius remained in the Po valley. He still refused to participate in any action against Antonius. Indeed, nothing could have been more favorable to his ambitions than the military deadlock in Gaul. The Senate was again helpless, and he was the only man in Italy who commanded an army. By the middle of June it was known in Rome that Octavius was thinking of a consulship. In the Senate no one could be found to propose that he should be allowed to stand for it, and Cicero, who still thought of himself as the young man's principal mentor, took pains to explain that he had been led astray by unscrupulous advisers. Of such, Octavius surely had no need in order to formulate his plans. If he was to negotiate with Antonius in the future, it would be highly advantageous to do so from a position not only of equal strength, but also of equal political eminence (what the Romans called *dignitas*). Antonius had held the consulship, by virtue of which he had entered Rome's most venerable political class—that of the consulars, or former consuls. A consulship would raise Octavius to the same exalted level of political prestige.

In July a delegation of centurions and soldiers from the army of Octavius appeared in Rome to demand from the Senate the consulship for their general and bonuses for his entire army. They also demanded that the law declaring Antonius a public enemy should be rescinded. When the news was brought back to Octavius that all demands had been rejected, he led his army of eight legions and supporting units across the Rubicon, the stream which separated Cisalpine Gaul from Italy, and marched on Rome. The Senate vacillated between measures of compliance and resistance as Octavius approached. On his arrival, it gave way

27

entirely. On August 19 of the year 43 B.C., Octavius and his cousin Pedius were elected consuls at a special election. This was the first of the thirteen consulships which Octavius would hold in the course of his long career. It was characteristic of Octavius that he kept his army outside the pomerium, the sacred boundary of the city, according to republican tradition and that on the day of his election he absented himself from the polls in order not to exercise undue influence in his own behalf. He had a nice feeling for appearances. It was also characteristic that he seized the public treasury and from it immediately began to reward his troops. He had a strong feeling for reality too, and there is no more urgent reality for one who depends on military support than well-paid soldiers.

One of his first acts as consul was to arrange for his adoption by Julius Caesar through a law passed by the curiate assembly. Now the slightest doubt could no longer exist concerning the legality of his position as Caesar's son. According to the Roman system of nomenclature, a man, when adopted, took the name of his adoptive father, but added to it his own family name with the suffix *anus*. Consequently, either by the testamentary adoption, if it was valid and complete, or by the law of the curiate assembly, Octavius became Gaius Julius Gaii filius Caesar Octavianus. As we have seen above, Octavius wished to identify himself as Caesar's son and never used the name Octavianus. To himself and his friends he was simply Caesar. It is a useful convention to call him Octavian and thus to distinguish him from his adoptive father until the point in his career when he was given the name Augustus. We shall make use of this convention from now on.

A special court set up under a law proposed by Pedius, the consul, placed the murderers of Caesar under interdiction; that is, they were deprived of the protection of the law. Octavian's task was now to take vengeance upon them, but he was incapable of doing so alone. Brutus and Cassius had collected large forces in the East which would have to be defeated in battle. Antonius commanded the largest army in the West. Both Plancus and Pollio had come over to him with their legions. The time had come for Octavian to come to terms with him.

Octavian met with Antonius and Lepidus near Bononia. The three men determined that the form in which they would exercise absolute power would be a commission consisting of themselves, appointed by law for the purpose of establishing public affairs (*triumviratus rei publicae constituendae*). It was further agreed that Antonius and Octavian would conduct a campaign against Brutus and Cassius while Lepidus remained in charge at Rome. In the division of the provinces Octavian's somewhat inferior position in the triumvirate was made clear. Antonius received Cisalpine Gaul, from which he could control all of Italy. He could could also draw on the resources of the new province of northern Gaul which had been established by Caesar's conquests. Lepidus' share comprised the old Roman province of Gallia Narbonensis and all of Spain. Africa, Sicily, Sardinia, and Corsica had been left to Octavian. Even to reach any part of these provinces he would have to run the risk of being captured by Sextus Pompeius, the son of his father's old enemy, Pompey the Great, whose fleet now dominated the western Mediterranean. But at the moment Octavian was in no position to protest. When Brutus and Cassius were defeated, the situation could be reviewed.

All three men were badly in need of funds, so they decided to proscribe their enemies and confiscate their estates. Antonius was also moved by a violent hatred of the senatorial group which had attempted to thwart his ambitions at every turn. Since the autumn of 44, Cicero had been the acknowledged leader of Antonius' opponents and in the famous orations known as the *Philippics* had excoriated him with every resource of his incomparable eloquence. He had refused to countenance any compromise in the Senate's dealings with Antonius, and where others had hesitated or trimmed, he had insisted that Antonius should be proclaimed a public enemy and treated as such. Without the weight of Cicero's influence, the Senate might never have had the courage to make war on Antonius. For the latter, the hour of revenge had finally arrived.

Octavian was deeply in Cicero's debt. It was largely Cicero who had persuaded the Senate to legalize Octavian's command of the army which he had privately raised, who had assuaged the doubts of many senators regarding the reliability of Caesar's son; and who had guaranteed the loyalty of Octavian to the Senate and his true republican sentiments. Octavian pleaded for Cicero's life without success when the first list of the proscribed was drawn up. He even demanded concessions from the two others which he thought they would never make. But he underestimated Antonius' fury. In return for Cicero's life, he added the name of an uncle to the list; Lepidus added that of a brother. Both were allowed to escape.

Even before their position was legalized, the triumvirate sent instructions to the Consul Pedius in Rome to have seventeen of the most important proscribed executed immediately. Cicero was among them. He faced death calmly on December 7, 43, after several halfhearted attempts to escape to Brutus in the East. By order of Antonius, his head and hands were displayed on the rostra in the Forum. This was only one of the abominable sights that met the eye in Rome in the course of the blood bath in which three hundred senators and two thousand knights lost their lives. Octavian, it is said, was even more ruthless than his colleagues in carrying out the proscription which he had first opposed.

After the soldiers had approved the terms of the agreement worked out near Bononia—they were amply rewarded in one of them—Octavian hurried back to Rome, where Antonius and Lepidus soon joined him. On November 27, on the proposal of the tribune Publius Titius, a law was passed which gave the triumvirate its legal powers. For a period of a little over five years (until December 31 of the year 38), the triumvirs were made superior to all the regular magistrates of the Roman state, whom they were given the power to nominate, and were accorded the right to make laws. Octavian had come a long way since the spring of 44, when he had landed in Italy a private citizen and resolved to accept the name of Caesar and his share of Caesar's estate.

The next section of the *Res Gestae* reads as follows. "I drove into exile by court action the men who butchered my parent and avenged their crime; later when they made war on the state, I defeated them twice in pitched battle." The two engagements were fought near the town of Philippi, in Macedonia. Although the ending of the first was indecisive, it cost the republicans the life of their most competent general, Cassius, who committed suicide when the part of the army which he commanded met defeat. In the second (October 23, 42), the forces of Brutus were routed, and their general took his own life. The principal murderers of Caesar were now dead, and the grim deed of the Ides of March was avenged. But the chief avenger had been Antonius. The victory was due to his skillful leadership on the field and to his personal valor. In fact, Octavian had been prevented by illness from any active participation in the first engage-

31

ment and had barely escaped with his life when Brutus stormed his camp. In the future Octavian would have to prove his ability as a general.

After Philippi, Antonius and Octavian redivided the provinces and the troops. Lepidus had proved himself ineffectual and was reduced to a subordinate position. While Antonius went off to the East to raise more money for the soldiers, Octavian returned to Italy to undertake the hateful task of settling the discharged veterans in Italian municipalities. This meant dispossessing the original inhabitants and alienating large segments of the population. The brother, Lucius, and the wife, Fulvia, of Marcus Antonius exploited the discontent to make trouble for Octavian and thus to promote the cause of Marcus. It would not do to let Octavian have his own way easily in Italy. Lucius raised troops and openly defied Octavian. The latter besieged Perusia (modern Perugia, in central Italy), where Lucius and his army had taken refuge. A famine of such intensity that it became proverbial finally forced Lucius to capitulate (February, 40). Octavian was forced to pardon Lucius and his army, for he was not prepared to fight a decisive war with Marcus. Octavian's position in the triumvirate gave him the opportunity to increase his strength, and his uneasy alliance with Antonius would have to be continued for some time, even at the cost of disagreeable concessions. But Octavian also had to show that he was a person whose indulgence could not be taken for granted. The penalty paid by Perusia for assisting Lucius was made a warning to other Italian towns: its leading citizens were brutally slaughtered, and the town was pillaged and burned.

A fundamental division of the Roman world was made between Octavian and Antonius at Brundusium in October, 40. Warfare had then seemed almost inevitable, but the soldiers on both sides had been in no mood to begin another civil war and had insisted on a peaceful settlement. In the pact which was made Antonius received the East and Octavian the West. Lepidus was given Africa. This arrangement left Octavian master of Italy with the resources of Gaul and Spain behind him. Italy had produced the soldiers who had created the Empire, and from Rome the Empire had been governed. It would be Octavian's task during the following years not only to increase his military strength but also to emerge as the champion of Rome and Italy around whom they would rally if any attempt was made from the East to impair their ancient sovereignty. Octavian needed time to consolidate this position. It was imperative that Antonius should be prevented from taking any hostile actions against him in the immediate future. To seal the new agreement, a dynastic marriage was celebrated between Octavia, the sister of Octavius, and Antonius. Octavian could hope that his sister would exert a restraining influence on her impetuous husband.

Sextus Pompeius still controlled the seas around Italy and could play havoc with the grain supply on which Rome depended. For lack of ships, Octavian could not move against him immediately. He was even compelled, in 39, to make humiliating concessions to Sextus in which Antonius joined him. Sextus was treated as an equal. The two triumvirs acknowledged his rule over Sicily, Corsica, and Sardinia, bestowed legal status on his pirates, and pardoned the proscribed who had fled to him. Property rights were flagrantly violated when the host of fugitive slaves who had joined his banners were declared free. Octavian must have seen that this arrangement would be of short duration. Nevertheless, he strengthened it by marrying Scribonia, the sister of the father-in-law of Sextus. She was his senior and had already been twice married. She bore him his only child, Julia, and he then promptly divorced her.

Sextus soon returned to his piracy. There was only one person to whom Octavian could appeal for the ships which he needed in order to defeat Sextus, and he was Antonius, who possessed a considerable fleet. Antonius offered naval assistance, but at a price. He was planning to follow in Caesar's footsteps by mounting a large-scale expedition against Parthia and needed to increase his army. The pact of 40 B.C. had given him the right to recruit in Italy, but he could not practically do so without the co-operation of Octavian. Octavian could provide troops. But, by the time Antonius appeared with his ships (autumn of 37), Octavian had constructed his own fleet. He was no longer dependent on Antonius and at first refused to meet him. Again warfare seemed imminent, but Octavia intervened and reconciled her husband and brother. The bargain which was struck was apparently very advantageous to Antonius. For 120 ships, he received 4 legions. The ships, however, were delivered immediately. The legions were to be sent later.

The triumvirs had continued to exercise their extraordinary powers after December 31, 38, because there had been no one to challenge them. They were recognized as *de facto* masters of the parts of the Roman world which they had assigned themselves. To Antonius this was probably satisfactory, but the situation in Italy was far different. Rome had a long tradition of constitutional government, and anyone who wanted to stand forth as the leader and champion of Italy had to wield power which was sanctioned by law. Octavian had the life of the triumvirate extended until the last day of 33.

The elimination of Lepidus took place soon after the naval

34

engagement off Naulochus, in Sicily, in which Octavian's fleet under Marcus Agrippa defeated that of Sextus Pompeius (September 3, 36). Lepidus had been invited to participate in the Sicilian campaign against Sextus and had crossed over from Africa with fourteen legions. After the defeat of Sextus, Plinius Rufus, who was commander of the Sextian forces on land, surrendered his eight legions to Lepidus. Relying on these considerable forces, Lepidus decided that the time had come to emerge from a position of humiliating subordination and to recover his equality in the triumvirate. He laid claim to Sicily by right of conquest and ordered Octavian, who was, in person, commanding his land forces, which were far inferior in numbers, to evacuate it. In doing so, he vastly overestimated his own qualities of leadership, misjudged the temper of his conglomerate army, and ignored one of his opponent's most powerful weapons—his proven ability to win over the minds and hearts of soldiers. Octavian addressed himself to this weapon with skill and courage. He not only sent agitators among Lepidus' troops, but, in an act of bravery which almost cost him his life, he rode into Lepidus' camp to persuade his soldiers to defect. He knew that they were sick of fighting and that Lepidus enjoyed little popularity among his old or new troops. The risk was well calculated. Mass defections ensued, and Lepidus, stripped of his military power, was forced to implore mercy.

Octavian showed clemency. First of all, he could afford to do so, since Lepidus had proved by his incompetence that he could not be dangerous in the future. Then, this was an occasion to demonstrate that the grim days of the proscriptions and Perusia were over. Lepidus forfeited his membership in the triumvirate but escaped with his life. He continued to be pontifex maximus until his death in 13 B.C. It was a priesthood that was held for life, and Octavian did not believe in tampering with sacred traditions.

Now that the fiction of Lepidus as an equal had totally vanished, many a Roman must have foreseen and dreaded the future. There was the example still fresh in many minds of the turn taken by events after the death of Crassus (53 B.C.), when the so-called first triumvirate was reduced to two members—Pompey and Caesar. It had taken a cruel civil war, which culminated in the battle of Pharsalus, to decide which of the two would be master of the Roman world. Now again supreme power was shared by two men who had divided that world between themselves. By its very nature such a situation could not last indefinitely. It would inevitably lead to a struggle for the undisputed supremacy of one or the other. It was impossible to envisage Caesar's son withdrawing peacefully before any other Roman on earth; it was equally impossible to imagine the ambitious and violent Antonius accepting a second place. It could only be hoped that for reasons of immediate interest, both men would be content for a while with their positions of equality.

Octavian was not one to miscalculate the future. It was more imperative than ever that he should have Rome, Italy, and the western provinces solidly behind him when matters came to a head. The first thing, however, was to show that he was absolute master of his own army. After the victory over Sextus, the soldiers had demanded bonuses in cash and land and had refused to be put off with promises. When rioting occurred, Octavian did not hesitate to act boldly. He even gave a dishonorable discharge to the soldiers of an entire legion. On the other hand, veterans who had been kept unreasonably long under the standards were dismissed with cash or an allotment of land.

When discipline had been restored, Octavian returned to Rome, where he was greeted with wild enthusiasm. His first act was to deliver a speech to the Senate and the people in which he reviewed his achievements and proclaimed the beginning of a new era of peace and prosperity, now that the civil wars had come to an end. To give a practical significance to his words, he canceled certain debts owed by private individuals to the state and reduced the burden of taxation. Among the honors which he accepted were an ovation, the transformation of the day on which he had defeated Sextus Pompeius into an annual religious holiday, and a gilded column in the Forum surrounded by the beaks of the ships which he had captured from Sextus and surmounted by a statue of himself. An inscription declared that he had re-established the peace, which had long been disturbed, on land and sea. Some years were destined to pass before the *pax Augusta* became a stable reality. But the seed of the idea which was later to play so large a part in the Augustan climate of thought was then sown in men's minds. Octavian's person was also declared sacrosanct or inviolable, an attribution to which we shall return when we discuss his political powers as Augustus.

The Roman people and Italy in general had good reason to be grateful to Octavian. With the defeat of Sextus, grain was again flowing in normally from overseas. The army was under firm control, and the citizens' financial obligations to the state had been lightened. There could be no doubt that Octavian was devoting himself entirely to the best interests of his fellow Romans in their own country, while Antonius was turning his back on them in a most un-Roman manner.

Cleopatra VII Philopator had come to Rome in the summer of 47 B.C. with her second husband, Ptolemy XIII, who was also her brother, and her son, usually called Caesarion,

37

whom she had born to Julius Caesar. She had been installed as Caesar's *maîtresse en titre* in a villa which he owned on the right bank of the Tiber. Caesar had met her in the autumn of 48 in Alexandria, in Egypt, where he had gone in pursuit of Pompey after the latter's defeat at Pharsalus. He was captivated by her and stayed on to defend her throne against her first husband and brother, Ptolemy XII, and the local population. She was a direct descendant of the great Ptolemaic kings who had ruled Egypt since the death of Alexander the Great (323 B.C.) and was fully aware of her position as queen and goddess in the eyes of the Egyptians. To the Romans she was a client-queen, officially a "friend and ally of the Roman people," for so Caesar had declared her. Members of the senatorial aristocracy resented her regal ways and looked with apprehension on her influence over the most powerful man in the Roman state. After Caesar's assassination, she returned hastily to Egypt.

It is likely that, as Caesar's friend and lieutenant, Antonius first met her in Rome. We do not know whether he then felt the fascination which had made Caesar, whose roving eye was notorious, her permanent and presumably faithful lover. The attraction certainly did not lie in sheer physical beauty, as Plutarch knew and we ourselves can perceive from portraits on coins and a marble head in the Vatican Museum, if the latter has been correctly identified. But her conversation was brilliant, and her person was surrounded by an aura of irresistible charm. She had a manly talent for government, was an accomplished linguist, and could advise as well as please. She knew the art of conquest through compliance and she could so combine the facets of her versatile nature as to appear the kind of woman that a particular man most desired. The Romans who hated and feared her have left us many reports of her wantonness. In fact, she seems to have had only two lovers throughout her life, and fierce ambition rather than unruly passion seems to have dictated her choice.

At the death of Caesar, she was in need of another Roman who, under her influence, would keep Egypt from being reduced to a Roman province. Her opportunity came in 41 when Antonius, who was collecting money in Asia Minor after the battle of Philippi, summoned her to Tarsus to answer the charge that she had aided Cassius. She must have been aware of Antonius' rather coarse tastes and his propensity for the spectacular. Her triumphant progress up the river Cydnus on a golden barge, as described by Plutarch, gave Shakespeare the material for one of his most glistening passages. Cleopatra acted as if she were the summoner and Antonius the summoned. He promptly fell in love with her and followed her to Egypt. Her new lover, however, unlike Caesar, was not the sole master of the Roman world.

For about four years (41–37), Antonius was occupied with other matters, some of which we have already mentioned. But when he returned to Cleopatra in 37, he showed the strength of his infatuation and at the same time began a series of acts which alienated large numbers of Romans. For in that year the astounding news was brought from the East that Antonius had married Cleopatra, recognized the twins which she had born him earlier as his legitimate children, and bestowed upon her considerable parts of the eastern Empire as a wedding gift. In Roman eyes the marriage could not have the slightest trace of legitimacy, since Antonius was still married to Octavia. Bigamy was not recognized by Roman law. To Cleopatra's subjects, and to many others in the East, Antonius had become her legitimate husband. In marrying her, Antonius had been merely exercising the privilege of Oriental monarchs.

Octavian must have weighed this news carefully. It was an unmistakable indication that under Cleopatra's influence Antonius was cutting his ties with Rome and was on his way to becoming an absolute monarch in the Hellenistic pattern. At home, an affair with Cleopatra would have been easily forgiven. No one expected stoic self-control from Roman generals overseas. But a formal marriage was a gratuitous insult to Roman sentiment. The presence of Antonius' legitimate wife, Octavia, at Rome, tending his home and raising his children, was a living rebuke to his behavior. Moreover, in humiliating Octavia, Antonius had indirectly shown his contempt for her brother.

Early in 35, word was brought to Rome of Antonius' successful campaign against the Parthians. The fact was, and Octavian knew it, that the expedition had been a miserable failure. Antonius had been compelled to beat a retreat into Syria and had lost thousands of his most experienced soldiers. He had now to redeem his honor in some other military adventure, and for that he needed more soldiers. He had been promised four legions from Italy by Octavian. When he sent for them, he received instead those of his ships which had not been destroyed in the war against Sextus. Octavian was already cutting him off from the source of the best soldiers. But with stubborn loyalty, Octavia insisted that her brother help her husband in some way. He sent her off to join Antonius with two thousand picked soldiers and some military supplies. For her pains she received a letter in Athens instructing her bluntly to return to Rome. This was the end of any hope for a reconciliation.

At the end of the next year (34), Antonius launched a violent attack upon Octavian as Caesar's son and heir. He proclaimed publicly in Alexandria that Caesar had been legally married to Cleopatra and that consequently their child Ptolemy Caesar (Caesarion) was Julius Caesar's legitimate son. The boy, according to Antonius, had been deprived of his rights, and he was doing no more than honoring Caesar's memory when he created him king of kings. Cleopatra as queen of kings was still to be his sovereign as well as his mother. On his own children by Cleopatra, Antonius bestowed whole provinces of the eastern Empire. In theory it could be said that he was acting within his rights in appointing a number of new client-kings who would rule their lands as Rome directed. In fact, he was establishing a new family dynasty with Cleopatra at its head. He further showed his scorn for Roman tradition by celebrating a triumph over Armenia in Alexandria. The triumphs of Roman magistrates were celebrated in Rome, and not abroad. A foreign queen could walk in one at Rome only as a captive; in the Alexandrian triumph of Antonius, Cleopatra presided.

The second five-year period of the triumvirate terminated on the last day of 33, and on January 1, 32, Octavian found himself a private citizen. The new consuls were friends and supporters of Antonius, and one of the first acts of one of them was to deliver a violent attack on Octavian in the Senate in his absence. Octavian replied by convening the Senate again, taking a seat between the consuls, and delivering a speech in his own defense. By these acts he made it quite clear that he did not intend to let the legal expiration of his triumviral powers affect his predominant position in Italy and the West. This part of the Roman world stood loyally behind him, as well as an army which he had hardened in campaigns conducted against the Illyrian tribes. Furthermore, he was armed with a knowledge of certain documents from the hand of Antonius which were certain to inflame the West against him when they were made public.

41

In one of them, Antonius had demanded that his official actions in the East, including his gifts to Cleopatra and his children by her, should be ratified by the Senate. The consuls of 32, foreseeing the resentment which would be caused by this high-handed alienation of Roman territory, refused to read the message. Octavian probably had it in mind when he stated at the end of his own defense that he would provide documentary evidence proving that Antonius was in the wrong and fixed a day for another meeting of the Senate. The consuls and about one-third of the senators who still supported Antonius realized that Octavian was now in a position to damn Antonius by his own words, and they left Rome to join him in the East. Octavian impeded the departure of no one. As the crisis approached, he wanted the lines cleanly drawn.

At a meeting of the remaining senators, Octavian presented his indictment. The outcome must have been disappointing to him. Negotiations with Antonius and a senate which he had constituted from the senators who had joined him dragged on. Then in May or June, Octavia received a letter from Antonius in which he formally divorced her. It broke the much-frayed family tie between the two leaders and caused a new wave of anger in the West against Cleopatra, who was naturally held responsible for the rupture. At about the same time, two Romans who had abandoned Antonius for Octavian informed the latter of the contents of the former's will, to which they had been witnesses. It had been placed in the safekeeping of the Vestal Virgins in Rome, which should have guaranteed its secrecy. Octavian, however, saw in it a trump card which he could not afford not to play at this juncture of events.

He seized the will and read it before the Senate and the people. In it, Antonius repeated that Ptolemy Caesar was the true son of Julius, bequeathed exorbitant legacies to his children by Cleopatra, and directed that if he should die in Rome, his body should be sent to Alexandria to be buried beside that of Cleopatra. The last provision caused particularly violent indignation. It seemed to confirm the apprehension among the Romans of Italy that if Antonius were victorious, Alexandria would supersede Rome as the capital of the Empire. In Rome, the time had finally come for decisive action. Antonius was stripped of all legitimate authority, but was not declared a public enemy. After the defeat of Sextus, Octavian had proclaimed that the period of civil wars was at an end. To maintain this fiction, war was formally declared against Cleopatra alone. Moreover, Antonius still had friends and supporters in Italy who might have hesitated to participate in a civil war against him. But no one could reasonably refuse to serve in a campaign against the hated foreign queen who, drunk with good fortune, was presuming to threaten the existence of the Empire itself. Finally Octavian was looking toward the future. When he had won his military victory, all Romans, regardless of the standards under which they had fought, would have to create again a single body politic under his leadership. Reconciliation and the healing of old wounds would be more readily effected if those who sided with Antonius did not receive the stigma of supporting a public enemy of the Roman state.

Since January 1, 32, Octavian's political actions had been carried out by virtue of his military power, his personal prestige, and his popularity as the acknowledged champion of the West. He held no magistracy and, as we have said above was legally a private citizen. There is no doubt that he could have had some extraordinary command bestowed upon him by a compliant Senate and people. He preferred a demonstration en masse of the solidarity of the West under his leadership. In the *Res Gestae* he describes it as follows: "All of Italy voluntarily swore an oath to me and demanded that I should be commander in the war that I won at Actium. The Gallic and Spanish provinces and the provinces of Africa, Sicily, and Sardinia swore the same oath. More than seven hundred Senators served under my standards of whom, up to the day on which this was written, eighty-three became consuls and about one hundred and seventy, priests."

The exact nature of this oath has been the subject of much discussion. Was it the usual military oath, extended to include the entire male adult population of the West and imposing upon it the obedience and other obligations which a soldier owed to his commander? Or was it more like the general oath, in which all adult male citizens annually swore their loyalty to later emperors? From the order of events in the passage of the *Res Gestae,* it seems more likely that a general oath of allegiance was first sworn, after which the people demanded that Octavian should lead them into war. But be that as it may, Octavian had demonstrated to the world that the entire West was solidly behind him and had received the moral support which increased his confidence and hastened actual warfare.

Antonius and Cleopatra passed the winter of 33–32 at Ephesus equipping the fleet which they intended to use against Octavian. The presence of the "foreign queen" in the camp of Antonius was a serious embarrassment. There were many Romans who were profoundly loyal to Antonius and were prepared to follow him into a civil war as a Roman general leading fellow Romans in an attempt to settle a Roman quarrel. But Cleopatra blurred, if she did not entirely distort, this simple concept of the situation. Her position as Antonius' wife, her important contributions to the

impending campaign, and, above all, her personal participation in its preparation created the aspect of an attack
by a foreign monarchy on Rome and Italy. Apart from the
usual number of pure opportunists whose only anxiety was
caused by the fear of not having chosen the winning side,
not a few more honorable men began to feel qualms and
hesitations about a loyalty which could not help serving
Cleopatra's political ambitions. Moreover, her deep in-
volvement in the campaign prevented Antonius from making the first obvious military movement—an invasion of
Italy before Octavian had raised sufficient naval forces to
put up effective resistance. Antonius still had friends and
supporters at home. But there could be no doubt that they
would rally around the standards of Octavian to defend
Italy against an attack in which a foreign enemy took part.

Well-wishers advised Antonius more than once to remove
Cleopatra from his headquarters. He realized the validity
of their arguments and once brought himself to the point
of ordering her to return to Egypt. In the clear knowledge
that she had become indispensable to his plans, she refused
to withdraw. She had come to Ephesus with two hundred
ships and was paying the joint forces from her own treasure
and feeding them with the grain of Egypt. She had determined to stake everything on the final hazardous throw
which might make her empress of Rome and the Mediterranean world, and she was not a person to stand idly by while
another, even her lover Antonius, decided how her fortune
should be risked. She had become a full partner in the great
adventure and had resolved to see it through in person. She
was with Antonius in his camp at Actium when the war
came to a showdown.

The army of Octavian landed in western Greece early in
31. In that year Octavian was consul and possessed the legal

powers and authority of the magistracy. He was again the rightful commander of his troops. Antonius had already taken up a position on the Gulf of Ambracia, where the two armies confronted each other. In the course of the summer, neither one was able to win a decisive engagement, but the advantage in the stalemate lay with Octavian. His fleet managed to cut off Antonius' supply of Egyptian grain. Moreover, Antonius was plagued by constant desertions, particularly of client-kings who defected to Octavian with their entire forces. On the insistence of Cleopatra, it was decided to seek the issue at sea.

On September 2, the naval engagement took place which is known as the battle of Actium. In it, the fleet of Octavian under the command of Agrippa won a decisive victory. Of the four hundred warships with which Antonius had sailed out to do battle, only some forty managed to escape. One of them carried Antonius and Cleopatra back to Egypt. Antonius' land forces surrendered soon thereafter. The West had triumphed over the East, and Rome and Italy had maintained their old supremacy. The deed had been done under the leadership of Octavian, and there was now no one alive within the Mediterranean world who could contend with him in force of arms, personal authority, and glory.

The war was virtually over, but there were still loose ends to be tied. Octavian badly needed the treasure of Egypt to reward his troops. In the winter of 31–30, the veterans who had been shipped back to Italy rioted, and Octavian was compelled to return there from Samos to quiet them with cash, land, and promises to share the booty of Egypt with them when it fell into his hands. In the meantime, Cleopatra undertook to collect new treasure. She killed and confiscated ruthlessly and did not even spare her country's most holy shrines. This wealth was placed in a mausoleum which she had built for herself. Beside it was laid material which could be easily set on fire and cause a general conflagration. She was well aware of Octavian's financial distress and did not intend to alleviate it without a price. The price was to be the bestowal of the crown of Egypt on one of her sons.

At Octavian's approach in the summer of 30, Egyptian resistance began to melt away. Antonius engaged in a few delaying actions, but was finally abandoned by his troops and committed suicide. Alexandria surrendered on August 1. Cleopatra was taken prisoner by a ruse and the treasure secured unharmed.

Our ancient sources tell us that Octavian set great store on having Cleopatra adorn his triumph at Rome, that he took every precaution to prevent her from committing suicide and dangled false hopes for her future and that of her children before her eyes to encourage her will to live, and, finally, that he was seriously put out when she outwitted him by bringing death upon herself. We can well believe that the Roman population was looking forward with malevolent joy to seeing the hated and presumptuous foreign queen walking in chains before their leader's chariot. It was a spectacle which Octavian owed to Rome and all those who had stood firmly behind him. While Cleopatra was alive and under his power, it would be difficult for him not to fulfill the expectations of the capital city.

But there was also the reverse of the medal. Cleopatra had been his adoptive father's mistress, lived with him in Rome, and born him the only son of his loins. Caesar had had her statue in gold—the precious metal indicated that she was divine—placed in the temple in his forum, which he had built and dedicated to Venus Genetrix. It stood there as a tangible reminder of Caesar's attachment to her. If Octavian brought Cleopatra to Rome to take part in his tri-

umphal procession, the next step—and it would be expected
and demanded by the people—would be her ignoble death
at the hands of the public executioner in the Mamertine
prison. Octavian would be ultimately responsible for it. He
must have foreseen that when a calmer mood prevailed, his
critics would have not a little to say about the curious kind
of filial piety which permitted a son to put to death the
woman whom his honored father had loved and respected.
Yet Octavian could hardly keep her in confinement the rest
of her natural life. Even if he was willing to defy public
opinion at Rome, psychologically, her death alone would
write a satisfactory finis to the last great war and the period
of civil strife in which she had been so deeply involved.

In view of these considerations it seems likely that the
news of Cleopatra's suicide gave Octavian a welcome feeling
of relief. Her pride and dignity would not allow her to suffer
the humiliation which awaited her in Rome. She had no drop
of humble blood in her veins, and she died in a manly fashion. By order of Octavian, she was given a royal burial, and
her body was laid to rest beside that of Antonius. She was
thirty-nine at the time of her death and the last Ptolemy
to rule over Egypt. It became a Roman province.

Two brutal pieces of business remained to be done, and
Octavian attended to them quickly. Antonius had left seven
children by his three wives. The eldest, Antyllus, his son
by Fulvia, had been designated as his heir and successor.
Octavian could not permit him to survive as a rallying point
for any future opposition. He was executed. All the other
children, including those by Cleopatra, were brought up by
Octavia. Caesar's son by Cleopatra presented an even more
urgent problem. In killing him, Octavian would be killing
Caesar's flesh and blood. But there could be only one living
Caesar, and the young man was put to death. Now, in the

autumn of the year 30 B.C., at the age of thirty-three, Gaius Julius Caesar, the son of the deified Caesar, was the undisputed master of the Roman world. The ascent to absolute power had largely been made by force of arms. The task of the future was to use this power wisely in the service of peace.

# III

# THE NEW ORDER

*The Emperor*

IT MUST HAVE BEEN CLEAR to everyone except the blindest and most stubborn traditionalists that the old republican form of government had failed miserably. Certainly it was clear to Octavian. The civil wars in which he had personally taken part were the culmination of a long period of disorder which the existing government had been helpless to prevent. Something would now have to be devised which would satisfy realistically the needs of Rome and her empire and maintain and strengthen the peace which Octavian had finally achieved. The obvious solution of the problem was to establish some form of absolutism. It was also the easy one, since after Actium and Egypt, Octavian possessed the power to make himself an absolute monarch. Moreover, it is highly probable that the majority of the common people of Rome would have been quite content to see him occupy a political position which assured him a completely free hand in carrying out measures from which they would presumably benefit.

To establish an absolute monarchy, however, regardless of benevolent intent, would have meant a drastic break with Roman tradition and an arousing of the hostility of a class of men whose active co-operation and good will Octavian would need in the future. The Senate had long been the governing body of Rome. It had occasionally been reduced to impotence in periods of civil strife, or had been dominated by individuals such as Sulla and Caesar. But it was the repository of a great tradition, and although its splendor had been tarnished, it was still Rome's most important organ of traditional government. It also represented the city's political and social aristocracy. What was left of the great families whose members had directed the destinies of the city during centuries of the Republic still sat in the Senate, along with a more recent nobility created by "new men," like Cicero, who had risen to the consulship by virtue of their own abilities and thus had conferred high station on themselves and their descendants.

In the late Republic, the Senate was composed of magistrates and former magistrates, and admission to it was gained by election to the quaestorship, the lowest rung in the ladder of high magistracies. In theory, the Senate was an advisory body which gave advice to the magistrates, who might or might not accept it. It could make resolutions (*senatus consulta*) which had behind them the weight of its great prestige, but only the people could turn them into laws. In fact, since the magistrates were all senators, they were not likely to flaunt the considered advice of their senatorial colleagues, and in many fields, such as the conduct of wars, foreign affairs, and the administration of the provinces, the Senate traditionally had the last word.

Although the people alone could make laws in their various assemblies, bills had to be conceived, deliberated, and drafted before they were presented for a vote, and this was one of the Senate's functions. Again, the people controlled admission to the Senate and determined the holders of the magistracies, since all of them, from the quaestorship up, were elective. But in the late Republic, elections had fallen

51

into such an infectious swamp of venality and corruption, had been so disturbed, broken up, or coerced by violence, or had turned in one way or another into a sordid traffic, that any semblance of honest electoral procedure had all but disappeared. This had too often resulted in the election of conspicuously unworthy and incompetent men who mismanaged and exploited Rome's interests at home and abroad for their own unscrupulous goals. Yet, in its long history the Senate had provided the civil and military leaders who had created Rome's greatness, and from its membership had come the magistrates and promagistrates who had administered the city and the Empire.

Confronted with *force majeure,* most senators would probably have acquiesced, at least temporarily, in a monarchy which deprived them factually of their old powers and privileges. But this would not mean that the republican feeling which was embodied in the Senate had been quenched. Octavian could recall that when the Senate had apparently become a docile instrument in Caesar's hands, republican convictions had moved a group of senators to assassinate him in the belief that he was aspiring to kingship. He had also seen the Senate reborn under Cicero's leadership and had watched its attempts to become again the state's governing body. Octavian could readily foresee that the senatorial class would eventually come to plague him if he did not treat it with the consideration which was its historical due.

But apart from the deference which was owed to the Senate because of its pre-eminent place in Roman history and the republican constitution, and apart from the dangers which would arise if it was humiliated or ignored, there was nothing in the principle of senatorial rule to offend Octavian. The city and the Empire had been governed since the beginning of the Republic by a relatively small group of citizens belonging to the Senate. They had quite naturally attempted to perpetuate their power from generation to generation by wealth, influence, family ties, and dynastic marriages. For a long time they had served the state well and made its welfare their paramount interest. But during the last century before Actium, they had failed to do so, both through an inability to cope with new problems and a deterioration of moral standards.

Octavian who, by blood, but chiefly by adoption, had his roots in this elite, could hardly feel any hostility toward its existence, provided that it took its responsibilities as seriously as its honors and privileges. He would need a great deal of loyal and efficient assistance to solve the political and administrative problems which faced him. A rehabilitated Senate, enjoying enough independence to respect itself, and be respected, and collaborating in a new program through patriotism as well as self-interest, could become a strong right arm.

It could become even more. In leading Rome and the West against Antonius and Cleopatra, Octavian had led freedom against tyranny in the eyes of his local followers. He could hardly make a travesty of his recent position by assuming the role of a Hellenistic monarch. The Senate, the magistracies which were entwined with it, and the popular assemblies had all been fundamental parts of the government of the Republic. The Senate in particular symbolized the old order and the *mores maiorum* (the ways of the ancestors), which were not lightly discarded in Rome. Yet as a practical people, the Romans had known how to create new realities under old appearances and names. It was desirable to keep the old institutions alive to show that the great stream of Roman political tradition was still flowing in the familiar channel. A Senate which occupied an important position in the government of the future would be the most striking proof of a return to tradition. At the same time Rome could not be allowed to fall to pieces again because of reverence for the past. If the old forms were kept, they would have to be made to serve the future. And a single hand of irresistible strength and authority would have to guide the whole.

From the purely practical point of view, the new order of government would have to be designed to accomplish the following purposes. First of all, the Empire had to be governed with maximum efficiency. Administration of the provinces was the field in which the old order had failed conspicuously. It was clearly no longer possible for the Mediterranean world to be ruled by a form of government that had been originally designed to administer the affairs of a city-state. The attempts to adjust it to the circumstances created by the Empire, as necessity or expediency dictated from time to time, had been ineffectual. The provinces could not be allowed to continue as areas of exploitation, subject to the whims, incapacity, or greed of governors who were sent out simply because they had held city magistracies. The provinces deserved competent and honest governors whose actions could be strictly supervised by an authority which they respected.

Next, the boundaries of the Empire as a whole had to be defended effectively. This could only be done by a standing army under a unified command. The period of extraordinary commands created to meet military emergencies had to be terminated. No general in the future should be able to march on Rome to seize power with an army that theoretically belonged to the Roman people but in fact had become a private expeditionary force.

Finally, Octavian had determined early in his regime that

the city of Rome should be elevated to the position which was its due as capital of the Empire and center of a new intellectual and moral movement. This meant more than undertaking a building program which would merely embellish the city and allow it to stand high in monumental beauty among the other great cities of antiquity. Wherever possible, the new buildings should reflect and promote the ideas and sentiments of the new order. Moreover, it was imperative that in Rome, more than in any other place, the façade of traditional republican government should be kept The city was the custodian of the institutions which had been created within its boundaries and could not be deprived of them without losing the most vital part of its historical identity. Rome without magistrates, a senate, and a voting body of free citizens would be a mockery.

Octavian perceived with shrewd political insight that the inauguration of his new order would be most effective if it was made in the form of a dramatic gesture. It had to be impressed on the Roman people by one huge act of renunciation that the period of extraordinary powers was at an end and that constitutional government in its familiar form had been given back to Rome and the Empire. Consequently, on January 13, 27 B.C., Octavian went before the Senate and performed the act which he thus describes in his own words: "In my sixth and seventh consulships [28 and 29 B.C.], when I had terminated the civil wars, having attained supreme power in all matters by universal consent, I transferred the Republic from my rule to the authority of the Senate and the Roman people." This was the official version of which we find echoes on the coins and in the inscriptions and literary works of the period. But like many official versions before and since, it is too simple, too sweeping, and not a little misleading. It tells us of a restored republic, but not how that republic was made to function. For this, detailed arrangements had to be made.

They had evidently been planned well in advance by Octavian, in consultation with his personal advisers and leading members of the Senate. For without debate, the Senate approved the following settlement on the same day on which the Republic was restored.

Octavian retained command of the provinces which needed to be heavily garrisoned for protection against a foreign enemy or could serve as bases of military operations. They were Syria, which bordered on the Parthian Empire, and Gaul, which faced the Germanic tribes across the Rhine. Northern Spain was added, since it had not been pacified. Egypt belonged to Octavian by right of conquest, and although it was nominally a Roman province, it was in a peculiar way Octavian's private property, as it had been that of the Ptolemies. Cilicia and the island of Cyprus completed the list. With these provinces, Octavian acquired command over the larger part by far of the Roman army. The other provinces, with their troops, were placed under the administration of the Senate.

The legal basis of Octavian's vast command seems to have been a decree of the Senate, made into a law by action of one of the popular assemblies, conferring upon him a special imperium for the period of ten years. He thus possessed in his provinces the traditional powers of a republican governor, extended for an unusual length of time. Unusual too, though not unprecedented, was that Octavian continued to hold the consulship at Rome for this and the following three and one-half years, while governing his provinces through his personal representatives.

Three days after this first settlement, the Senate conferred a number of honors on Octavian. The most important was that henceforth he should be called Augustus. In the writers of the Republic, the adjective *augustus* is generally applied to a holy place, such as a temple, or to a holy act, such as augury. Octavian had been urged to accept the name Romulus as the second founder of the city. He had refused because of its connotations of kingship. The name Augustus surrounded him with an aura of sanctity and established a certain religious relationship with Romulus who, as augur, had founded Rome by holy augury (*augusto augurio*), according to the early poet Ennius. The title did not deify him, but placed him on a level which was somewhat above that of the purely human. Henceforth, we shall call him Augustus. At the same time it was decreed that the month *Sextilis* should be named *Augustus* in the Emperor's honor. The name of the previous month, *Quintilis,* had already been changed to *Julius* in honor of Julius Caesar. Hence our July and August.

Another honor paid to Augustus took the form of a gold shield which was placed near the altar of Victory in the new Senate house dedicated in 29 B.C. (the *Curia Julia*). It bore an inscription stating that the Senate and the Roman people had given it to Augustus because of his valor (*virtus*), clemency (*clementia*), justice (*iustitia*), and righteousness (*pietas,* which can also be translated as "sense of duty"). The "clemency" may make us wince when we recall the proscription of 43, to which Octavian subscribed, and the massacre at Perusia, for which he was solely responsible. The ancients themselves were forced to recognize a singular lack of mercy on the part of Augustus during the early years of his ascent to power. But be that as it may, the virtues on the shield are a manifestation of what the Romans expected from the first man in their state, the *princeps*.

Used as a substantive, the word meant "first man" or

"chief" and was a familiar republican term. It was applied to those men in the political life of the state who were acknowledged leaders because of their achievements and influence. They were the men whose opinions carried the greatest weight in the Senate and before the people. Almost all of them had risen to the consulship. Their power during periods when they did not hold a magistracy lay in their prestige. We find the term used loosely about members of the senatorial nobility who had not won any particular distinction by their own efforts. But in a stricter sense, high birth alone could not make a man a *princeps*. He himself had to win this position of respect and authority and demonstrate by his words and deeds that he was a leader. As is natural, at various times in the history of the Republic there were men who far surpassed their fellow *principes* in reputation, actual power, and influence. These were first citizens in the absolute sense of the word "first." The other *principes* continued to exist and to be so called. But by general consent, the outstanding *princeps* enjoyed a primacy among them.

Augustus applied this familiar republican term to himself in the *Res Gestae*. He uses it to indicate the period of time when we should say today that he "reigned" or "ruled." Obviously Augustus could not adopt any word which had the slightest monarchical connotation to indicate the many years when he held supreme power. Hence, we read "while I was *princeps*" or "before I was *princeps*." This, of course, was meant to convey that Augustus was no more than the first-chosen among his fellow citizens. He even speaks in the same document of other *principes* with the meaning "leading men." Augustus also made clear the foundation on which his primacy rested. To his description of the restoration of the Republic he adds, "After this time I excelled everyone in authority, but had no more power than any of my other

colleagues in the magistracies." "Authority" is a literal translation of the Latin word *auctoritas*. It meant to the Roman
the sum total of qualities in a man that commands respect
for his person and opinion. Birth, wealth, personal achievement, talent, and virtue all contributed to a Roman's *auctoritas*. It was his greatest extralegal source of influence and
power, and in connection with the *principes* of the Republic,
it was translated above as "prestige." In choosing the title
*princeps* to designate his position in the state and in em-
phasizing the equality of the power which he shared with
his colleagues in the magistracies, Augustus was asking his
fellow Romans to consider him one of a long line of republican *principes* who had functioned within the framework
of traditional government.

Although *princeps* soon became a usual designation for
the Emperor and we now generally refer to Augustus' form
of government as the Principate, it did not become a part
of the official imperial titulary. But *Imperator* was a different
matter, for in Augustus' use of that word we find the seed
of the meaning of our word "emperor," which is derived
from it. Under the Republic, any magistrate who commanded an army in the field with supreme and absolute
authority did so by virtue of the military command (*imperium militare*) which had been conferred upon him at
Rome. He was technically an *imperator,* but he had no
right to place the title behind his name until he had been
acclaimed *imperator* by his troops after a victory over a
foreign enemy. Such an acclamation was the prerequisite
of a triumph. But a general lost the military imperium on
crossing the sacred boundaries of the city of Rome (*pomerium*), except for the day of his triumph. When he had
lost his title of *imperator,* he did not reacquire it until he
received a new military command and had been reacclaimed

by his troops. He might then add the number of his acclamations to the title.

We are told by some of our ancient sources that in 45 B.C. Julius Caesar received the right to use *imperator* as the first of his three names (*praenomen*). This should mean that from Gaius Julius Caesar he became Imperator Julius Caesar. Furthermore, we are informed that this use of the title was accorded to his descendants. But the fact seems to be that Caesar never used *imperator* in this way and was content to abide by republican tradition, putting the title behind his proper name only in the periods between his acclamations and triumphs. It is also most unlikely that the new use of the title was made hereditary, even if it was voted at all.

Augustus was acclaimed *imperator* by his troops on April 15, 43, when he was fighting against Antonius at Mutina. Legally, he had the right to place the title after his name, where all Roman titles belonged, only until he entered Rome on August 19 of the same year. In the midst of this turbulent period, when powerful men were taking the law into their own hands, it is doubtful whether he observed this legal limitation. What we do know for certain is that his friend and general, Marcus Agrippa, who had been campaigning in Gaul, had coins struck in 38—probably in a Gallic mint—on which Augustus appears as "Imperator, Son of the Deified Julius," or "Imperator Caesar, Son of the Deified Julius." These are the earliest examples of *imperator* used as a *praenomen* or, at least, in the place where the *praenomen* habitually appears. From this time on "Imperator Caesar," with or without "Son of the Deified [Julius]," is found as the Emperor's name at the beginning of his titulary. After 27, "Augustus" was added as part of his proper name. Then there followed other titles, such as that

of the consulship, and among them *imperator,* in its old republican sense indicating military victories won by Augustus or his lieutenants in the field.

What was the significance of using *imperator* in this new
way? Did it remind the Romans that Augustus was the commander in chief of virtually all the Roman armed forces?
Or was it meant to suggest to them that here was the victorious general, par excellence, who took precedence over
all other victors? During the civil war there had been a spate
of *imperatores* and triumphs, and the proconsuls of the province of Africa continued to be saluted by their soldiers as
*imperatores* down to A.D. 22 (Contrary to the general rule,
Africa, although a senatorial province, continued to have
an army under its governor, a proconsul, in the Augustan
era.) The latter explanation is probably nearer to the truth.
At any rate, the word *imperator* had strong military connotations in the Roman mind, and it has been noticed that
Augustus began to use it less frequently as a *praenomen*
after he restored the Republic in 27 and wished to emphasize the civil nature of his functions. It appears in the *Res
Gestae* only as a military acclamation. But it was already
firmly fixed in popular usage, and although Augustus' immediate successors to the purple avoided its official use, except to indicate the victories of their forces among the other
titles which followed their names, from Vespasian (A.D. 69–
79) on for centuries to come, it stood first in the imperial
titulary with the connotations of supreme power contained
in our word "emperor."

In 23 B.C., another settlement was made between Augustus and the Senate. Through the consulship which Augustus
continued to hold from 27 to the middle of 23, he had the
power to take part in governing the senatorial provinces.
Their governors, chosen by the Senate from among its own

members who were former magistrates, were responsible to the Senate and its presiding magistrates, the consuls, of whom he was not only one, but also the most influential. Augustus, however, resigned the consulship on July 1, 23, and a way had to be found by which he could legally impose his authority on the senatorial provinces whenever he felt it to be in their best interests. The solution lay in changing the nature of the imperium granted to him in 27. The division of the provinces between Augustus and the Senate continued as a practical matter. But henceforth Augustus would govern his share by means of a proconsular imperium that was divorced from the consulship at Rome, which he had ceased to hold. Moreover, this imperium was made superior to the imperia possessed by all governors in all provinces. This would not, of course, affect the governors of imperial provinces who were appointed by Augustus and made responsible to him alone. But it would allow the Emperor to intervene legally in the affairs of senatorial provinces, since his imperium was greater (*maius*) than that of the senatorial governors.

There is abundant evidence that he did so especially to correct injustices under which the provincials suffered. If the Senate was slow to act, Augustus did not hesitate to give instructions to the governors of senatorial provinces by edict and to proclaim his own decisions. There is a revealing clause in an edict which has come down to us: Governors would do well to act in such and such a manner "until the Senate has deliberated on the situation or I have found something better." The reference to the Senate reminds the provincials that they are inhabiting a province administered by the Senate. The reference to himself makes it plain that he had the power to act independently as he was doing. We can be quite sure that the senatorial governors followed

Augustus' instructions to the letter and that after his decisions the Senate considered the matter closed.

In regard to the city of Rome, republican tradition did not allow a proconsul to exercise his powers within its sacred boundaries. In fact, he had to lay down his imperium before crossing them. It was plainly unthinkable that Augustus should be deprived of his power to govern the Empire because of his presence in the capital. Consequently, provision was made that he should not have to lay down his imperium on entering the city or have it renewed at his departure. This, however, did not solve the problem of his authority over city affairs. In meetings of the Senate the consuls would enjoy precedence. Apparently, in 23 B.C. Augustus was willing to see if the image of the republican government in Rome could function without his presence in the consulship. But the people protested against his withdrawal. The outcome was that, after Augustus had refused the dictatorship and the consulship for life, a compromise was reached in 19 B.C. by which he outwardly became the equal of the consuls of the year without holding the actual consulship. He sat between the consuls at meetings of the Senate, was attended by the same number of lictors, and possessed the rights of convoking the Senate at his pleasure, opening official business, and speaking whenever he pleased on any subject he chose.

From its creation in the fifth century B.C., the tribunate had been identified with the interests of the common people of Rome. From a purely plebian office, the function of which was to protect the plebeian from unjust or injurious treatment at the hands of a patrician magistrate, it had developed over the centuries into an integral and important part of the structure of Roman government. The tribunes could initiate or veto legislation. They sat in the Senate, presided over

63

the tribal assembly, and possessed the right to defend any citizen, patrician or plebeian, against an encroachment on his rights. Their power to arrest had even been used against the consuls. The person of a tribune was sacrosanct; that is, hands could not be laid upon him to restrain his actions.

Although Augustus devoted his first thoughts to the Senate, which had been the stronghold of the political nobility, he could not ignore the republican office which had been the bulwark of the rights of the people and of popular causes against the assaults of the ruling class. The common people, who, as a whole, had supported Augustus with enthusiasm, deserved some concrete evidence that he would serve as their protector and guardian throughout his life. The tribunate offered him a way to identify himself with the people's interests within the framework of the old constitution.

But there was an obstacle. As a patrician, Augustus could not hold the tribunate without violating an old tradition. Moreover, it was an office that was limited to a year and was inconsistent with some of Augustus' other powers, such as the proconsular imperium. Julius Caesar, however, also a patrician, had shown the way out of the difficulty. In 44, although he did not hold the tribunate, he had been given the sacrosanctity of a tribune. The same inviolability was conferred upon Augustus in 36 with the right to sit among the tribunes in the Senate. In 30, he received the tribune's right to come to the assistance of any citizen as far as the eighth milestone beyond the pomerium, a considerable extension of the traditional area of competence.

The final step was obvious. In 23, after he had resigned the consulship, Augustus received from the Roman people all the rights and powers inherent in the tribunate for life, without becoming a tribune. This tribunician power largely made up for what he had lost by resigning the consulship. In the Senate he could initiate or veto decrees, and he could also preside over the tribal assembly and propose or veto bills. His person had already been made sacrosanct, and he had been granted the right to protect his fellow citizens. But possibly of greater importance than these legal consequences of the tribunician power was the psychological effect upon the people at Rome. By accepting this new kind of tribunate for life, Augustus had proclaimed himself the champion of the interests of the people, the protector of the weak and humble. The value which he placed on the office is clearly demonstrated by the fact that from 23 on he numbered the years of his reign by the number of times he had held the tribunician power, calculated on an annual basis. Tribunes continued to be elected annually by the tribal assembly in good republican fashion. In principle, they possessed and performed the traditional rights and functions of the tribunate. But the people knew that henceforth Augustus alone would look after them.

The censorship for life was offered to Augustus in 22. He refused to accept it. He realized that his other powers enabled him to perform legally whatever censorial functions still needed to be performed—several of them had fallen into abeyance—and he was not inclined to assume an office unnecessarily which was both antiquated and unpopular. One of the chief duties of the republican censors had been to conduct a census of the Roman citizens every five years. Before 44 B.C., this task had fallen to the consuls. As consul in 28 B.C., and by virtue of a special grant of consular power in 8 B.C. and A.D. 14, Augustus, with or without a colleague, held censuses. He appears to have relied on the same consular authority in revising the senatorial rolls three times. This too had been a function of the censors.

Supervision of the public morality had also been a censorial function. The two censors, if they were in agreement, could even remove a senator from the Senate or a knight from the equestrian order, if, in their opinion, he had committed one of a number of acts which rendered him unworthy of his political and social status. Augustus tells us in the *Res Gestae* that he was thrice offered the guardianship, with supreme power, of laws and morals by the Senate and the Roman people (19, 18, and 11 B.C.) This he refused as contrary to traditional Roman custom. But he adds that he was able to accomplish what the Senate wished to have done through him by virtue of his tribunician power. He is referring to the reforms, many of them of a social and moral nature, which he established by laws passed by the tribal assembly.

In 12 B.C., on the death of Aemilius Lepidus, Augustus was elected pontifex maximus by such a multitude as Rome had never seen before. He thus obtained the highest priesthood in the state and became its most important representative in its relations to the gods. Ten years later the title of "father of his country" (*pater patriae*) was conferred upon him. The title was not new, and there are indications that it was applied to him informally many years before. Cicero had been acclaimed *pater patriae* after saving Rome from the Catilinarian conspiracy, and before him Marius had probably been honored in the same way. Among the honors which the Senate had heaped on Julius Caesar toward the end of his life was the title "parent of his country" (*parens patriae*). It proclaimed that Caesar was the protecting and beneficent father of the Roman people who sowed the seed of a new kind of *pietas* between the ruler and the ruled. In the ruler, it was devotion to the prosperity and happiness of his people, a sense of duty which obliged

66

him to deserve well of them. In the ruled, it was loyalty and obedience. When Augustus officially accepted the title "father of his country," he was acknowledging that the virtue of *pietas* which the Senate and people had placed hopefully upon his shield in 27 B.C. had become a political and emotional reality in the relations between himself and all other Romans.

We are now in a position to summarize Augustus' position in Rome and the Roman state after the restoration of the Republic. In regard to himself, he had preserved the old words and appearances of traditional Roman government remarkably well. From 27 to 23, he had exercised his power through the highest regular magistracy of the Republic, the consulate. He had been elected to it annually by the people, and regularly held it with a colleague. As consul, he had been charged with the administration of certain provinces. On laying down the consulate in 23, he received a proconsular imperium for ten years. This was an extension in area of competence and duration of time of the power by which republican governors had governed their provinces. In the late Republic too, certain generals had been granted an imperium superior to that enjoyed by the governors of other provinces. The tribunate was also an old republican office. When Augustus accepted its powers, he was accepting traditional powers under a different form, but even the form carried the popular name. He had refused extraordinary offices that were inconsistent with republican tradition: the dictatorship, consulship, and censorship for life. By obtaining old powers in modified or extended forms, he had apparently kept within the limits of the traditional constitution, and yet was in fact the supreme ruler of Rome and the Empire. Behind him, under his direct command, stood almost all of the Roman armed forces, and in dealing with individuals, or a group of individuals like the Senate, the pure weight of his *auctoritas* would determine any question in his favor. The restored Republic had acquired a constitutional monarch.

## *The Senate*

It is of no small significance that the consul who announced the death of Marcus Antonius to the people at Rome, and proposed to the Senate a number of measures dishonoring his memory, was Marcus Tullius Cicero, the son of the great orator. He had been proscribed with his father at the end of 43, but was already safely in Greece with the army of Marcus Brutus, in which he later fought at Philippi. After the defeat, he joined the forces of Sextus Pompeius in Sicily, returning to Rome in 39 by virtue of the treaty between the triumvirate and Sextus which provided an amnesty for the "Republicans" who had taken refuge with the latter. He entered upon his consulship on September 13, 30, and laid it down only a few weeks later. Yet, during this brief space of time he was the colleague of the man who subscribed to his father's death, for Octavian was consul for the fourth time during all of 30. After an interval of a few years, the younger Cicero became governor of Syria and then of Asia. He owed all his high offices to the good will of Octavian.

Ancients and moderns alike have held that in treating Cicero so generously Octavian was moved solely by the desire to make some compensation for the part which he had played in causing his father's death. Undoubtedly this was a factor. But we must also see in the younger Cicero's elevation to the consulship only a year after the battle of Actium a clear indication, given intentionally by Octavian, that members of the senatorial nobility would have a place in the future government of Rome, regardless of the part which they or their ancestors had played in the political struggles which followed Caesar's assassination. What we know of the younger Cicero as a man will not allow us to believe that Octavian was honoring him for his personal distinction. It was rather his father's name and memory which determined his elevation to the consulship. The elder Cicero had led the fight for constitutional government after the death of Caesar, and his valiant efforts had cost him his life. In the eyes of many, he was the embodiment of the old Republic and of a form of government in which the Senate had been the predominant element. The fact that his son had been made consul at the moment when Octavian had reached the peak of his power was a clear indication that Octavian was thinking in terms which boded well for the senatorial nobility.

Octavian soon showed in a more explicit way that he was concerned with restoring the Senate to its old prestige and with making it a useful and important instrument of government within the new order. By virtue of the censorial power which was inherent in the consulate, Octavian, while he was consul in 29 and 28 B.C., held a *lectio senatus* (a choosing of the Senate), a legal procedure by which unworthy members were eliminated from the body. In the disorder of the civil wars, many such men had managed to worm their way in, and the membership had grown to about one thousand. The manner in which Octavian conducted his first *lectio* was characteristic equally of the respect for the Senate as an institution which he displayed throughout his entire regime and his determination not to be thwarted by it. He first requested each senator to judge his own qualifications and to withdraw voluntarily if he found them wanting. The result was probably what Octavian expected: only fifty or sixty senators found themselves to be unsuitable members of the august body. Now more drastic measures were justified, and Octavian compelled one hundred and forty more to resign.

Ten years later, Augustus found the size of the membership still too unwieldy and within it a considerable number of undesirables. This time he contrived a complicated procedure involving selection by choice and by lot through which the Senate should purge itself. When this broke down, he intervened personally and reduced the membership to six hundred. Finally, in A.D. 4, the Emperor held his last *lectio*. On this occasion he was more successful in persuading the senators to do the work of elimination for him.

These were negative measures which corrected already existing conditions. Positive steps were far more difficult to take. From the time of Sulla (*c*.80 B.C.), admission to the Senate came to a man with the quaestorship, which was an elective office. Hence the electorate alone, composed of the great body of Roman citizens who resided at Rome or near enough to it to participate in elections, determined who would be the new senators. Once within the Senate, the new senator remained there for life, unless he was expelled for due cause. But with the quaestorship, his career as a senator had hardly begun. Ahead of him lay a number of magistracies, the tribunate, aedileship, praetorship, and consulship. Of these, only the last two would bring him political eminence and qualify him for high positions abroad. All these magistracies were also elective. So again the voters decided who should go up the ladder and how far.

It was clearly unthinkable under the restored Republic to suppress or seriously impair the people's age-old right to elect their own magistrates. This would have been tantamount to destroying or damaging one of the constitutional pillars of republican Rome. But could the voters and candidates be trusted to abandon the shameless electoral practices of the late Republic if given an entirely free hand? What steps could be taken so that acceptable candidates, at least, should stand for election and the people should seriously choose the best among them, especially for the higher offices where so much was at stake? To what extent and by what means could Augustus intervene to assure the election of the kind of men the state badly needed without using his actual power in a conspicuously monarchical way?

There were two acceptable ways, one traditional and the other legal, by which Augustus could influence the choice of the voters and help determine the kind of candidates from which they would choose. An old republican custom allowed any Roman, regardless of his political or social position, to campaign in behalf of a friend. Augustus, whenever he attended elections, circulated among the voters with his candidates and begged votes for them in the traditional way. He himself then voted as an ordinary citizen. In A.D. 8, he gave up active campaigns of this sort and merely posted the names of the candidates he recommended.

We do not know how many candidates Augustus supported in this way, or for what magistracies. We can assume however that only the lower magistracies were involved, where the Emperor's intervention would be less invidious, and that he never recommended as many candidates as there were posts to be filled. Rather, his commendation was probably a way of assuring the election of a few men, whose careers he had some good reason to promote, without closing the door to others.

During his consulships, Augustus had the right and duty

to scrutinize the list of candidates for all magistracies and to reject those he considered unqualified for the office they were seeking. We do not know how severely he acted in this capacity. Moreover, from the middle of 23 B.C. until his death, he held the consulship only twice, in 5 and 2 B.C. This does not mean that he did not make his aversions known to the consuls in office when he was not consul himself and that they did not prevent *personae non gratae* from standing. But we should be mistaken if we imagined that Augustus, as consul, or the other consuls admitted to candidacy only as many candidates as there were offices in a given year. In 8 B.C. the accusation was made that all magistrates from the consuls on down had been elected through bribery. Bribery is usually quite superfluous when each candidate is automatically assured of election.

From 27 to 23 B.C., when Augustus was annually one of the consuls, we hear of no electoral disorders. The Emperor probably let it be known unofficially whom he desired to have as his consular colleague each year, and the man was elected. When Augustus resigned his consulship in the middle of 23, he saw to it that his successor was a man whose very presence in the office was a reminder of the past and a renewed pledge that the differences of that past were forgotten. This man, Lucius Sestius, had fought on the side of Brutus at Philippi.

With Augustus in the city, the consuls for 22 were calmly elected. But the people were far from satisfied, for they had identified Augustus with the consulship and saw in it the most tangible evidence of his supremacy. As we have mentioned, they tried unsuccessfully to force the dictatorship on him in 22. Soon after his departure from Rome on imperial business in the East, trouble broke out. The people reserved one of the consulships for 21 for Augustus, but he declined. Two senators then stood for the vacancy and with their supporters brought back to the city some of the rioting that had characterized too many elections at the end of the old Republic. Augustus was naturally vexed. Here was the first proof that when he removed his guiding hand, the candidates and the people would return to their old license. Yet he refused to choose between the candidates and thus to assure the election of one of them. He adopted the course of ordering the election to be held in the absence of both candidates. This did not prevent disorder at the polls, but one of the men was finally elected.

In 19, there was a general repetition of these events. A consulship was reserved for Augustus; he refused it, and rival candidates and their factions caused bloody brawls. The Senate, in desperation, sent a delegation to the Emperor to implore him to intervene. This time he did so by appointing one of the delegates the second consul for the year. During his absence there had been other irregularities. An ambitious aedile won such popularity by extinguishing fires in private houses with his own slaves and at his own expense that the people not only voted to reimburse him but elected him praetor for the following year. This broke the law which forbade these magistracies to be held in consecutive years.

Augustus hurried back to Rome from Syria. He arrived in the city on October 12, 19. A relieved Senate voted to erect an altar to Fortuna Redux, the Good Fortune who had brought him back safely, to celebrate his return. He had experimented with completely free elections, and the experiment had failed. The people on the whole would probably have been quite willing to have him appoint the magistrates or to transfer the elections to the Senate. When the matter was left entirely in their hands, they had shown themselves incapable of acting with restraint and good judgment. And the candidates themselves were greatly to blame.

Augustus continued to preserve the old electoral façade, but curbed turmoil and violence. The bribery of voters continued, and the scandalous elections of 8 B.C., which we have mentioned, caused Augustus to demand in the future a deposit of money from each candidate which he would forfeit if he violated the election laws. The purging of the Senate in A.D. 4 shows that undesirables were still entering the Senate, or at least proving themselves incompetent or unworthy within the body.

The situation was not satisfactory. The voters elected the candidates recommended by the Emperor and then exercised their power of choice among the rest—not always wisely. The election of the right kind of praetors and consuls was becoming more crucial than ever. The Empire needed more and more administrators of praetorian and consular rank. In A.D. 2, the practice was established of electing two pairs of consuls, each of which would govern for half a year. This helped to meet the problem of quantity, but not of quality.

Finally, in A.D. 5, Augustus took the first step in radically reforming the old procedure of electing praetors and consuls. We have learned of it from a recently discovered document, the *tabula Hebana*. The details of the reform are not always clear, but a reasonable case can be made for the following interpretation.

A group of voters consisting of all of the senators, six hundred at that time, and three thousand knights, selected from the entire equestrian order in Italy, held a preliminary election of praetors, and consuls. The knights had been picked by Augustus to serve as jurymen and were personally indebted to him for the honor. Furthermore, this electoral group as a whole was divided into ten centuries, which bore in subdivisions of five each the names of the Emperor's two dead grandsons, Gaius and Lucius Caesar, whom he had intended to make his heirs. The very names of the subdivisions bound the group to the Emperor as a person. The group was small enough to be manageable and yet large enough to escape the reproach of being a mere imperial clique. The candidates chosen in this preliminary election then came up for final election by the centuriate assembly, bringing with them the public indorsement of the highest and most influential parts of the citizen body. Other candidates were permitted to run against them in the final election before the assembly, but, if any had the temerity to do so, their chances of success were slim indeed.

Thus, without destroying the people's right to elect their higher magistrates, Augustus had devised a way by which the voters virtually had to elect a given slate of candidates. The slate was chosen by a body of men who, presumably, had the interests of the state at heart and would carefully weigh the qualifications of each candidate for the high offices for which they were contending. But we can also be sure that the preliminary electoral body was discreetly informed of the Emperor's wishes, and showed their gratitude for past favors and their hope for future ones in voting the right way. A problem of Empire had finally been solved at the expense of the city electorate. First-class former magistrates would be available to command the legions and govern the provinces. As for the electorate, there is not the slightest indication that they resented the change.

Let us now look at the magistracies and their qualifications. On reaching their majority, around the age of sixteen, the sons of senators were enrolled in the equestrian order. They were permitted, however, as candidates for a senatorial career to wear the purple stripe (the *latus clavus*) on their tunics. This was a symbol of senatorial rank. They did not become actual senators until they were elected to the quaestorship. Young men of equestrian families might also be granted the right to wear the broad stripe by the Emperor, if he considered them worthy of contending for the quaestorship. This was one of the ways in which admission to the Senate was opened to men who had not been born into the senatorial circle. Although the Senate was to remain a political aristocracy, it was not to be closed to new blood. An equestrian youth who had received the broad stripe, but, like the poet Ovid, failed to stand for the quaestorship, forfeited his senatorial symbol and resumed the narrow stripe (the *angustus clavus*) of the order of his birth.

The offices which were prerequisites of the quarestorship were both military and civil. They included service in the army as junior officers and membership on one of a number of minor boards or commissions, administrative or judicial, which functioned in the city of Rome. Thus, a young man served his apprenticeship partly abroad in the Emperor's army and partly in Rome under the Emperor's eye. It was sound preliminary training, since a succcessful career in the future would involve magistracies at home as well as posts in the provinces.

The men who were admitted to candidacy for the quaestorship had to be twenty-five years old and had to possess a census (financial status) of 1,000,000 sesterces ($50,000). When a man who was qualified in other respects lacked the required sum, Augustus often made it up from his own purse. We know of a specific case in which he provided the full 1,000,000 sesterces, not only so that the man might have his seat in the Senate, but also that he might marry and have children. The person in question was the grandson of the famous Quintus Hortensius Hortalus (consul in 69 B.C.), who in oratory had been Cicero's most serious rival. Augustus' generosity is an example of the interest which he took in the descendants of the noble families of the Republic.

There were twenty quaestorships. At least half of the elected quaestors could hope to see service in the senatorial provinces as the principal assistants of their governors. At Rome two of those who had been recommended for election by the Emperor became his private secretaries. Each consul had two quaestors to help him with his official business. The rest were occupied with various administrative duties, including the supervision of the public archives. Under the Republic, two quaestors had been in charge of the public treasury. In 23 B.C., they were replaced by two praetors. The chief financial burden imposed upon the quaestors was the paving of the city streets. They shouldered it as a group.

In the Augustan Age, the ruling class was composed of members of patrician and plebian families. Centuries had passed since the highest magistracies were exclusively held by an aristocracy of blood. The plebian members stood on an equal footing socially with the patrician members of the political aristocracy, but they are not to be confused with the members of the plebs, the common people of Rome.

A few old distinctions had survived, especially in religious matters, which are notoriously impervious to change. Only patricians could occupy certain priesthoods and perform certain religious rites, but many patricians had been killed in the proscriptions and civil wars. Their reduced number was particularly embarrassing at a time when Augustus was planning to foster a revival of religious feeling and practice. Moreover, a semblance of balance between patricians and plebian members of the governing class had been struck in the Republic, and for the sake of form and sentiment it was desirable to maintain it. In 30 B.C., a law was passed giving Augustus the right to create new patricians. He made use of it in the following year.

In the early period of the Republic, the tribunes had led the plebians against the patricians in their fight for equal political rights. It was a vestige of this situation that no patrician could stand for the tribunate. Augustus made it a general rule that plebians should stand for either this office or the aedileship, if they intended to go on to the praetorship. There were ten tribunates and six aedileships to be filled annually. Thus, plebians who were former quaestors had sixteen positions open to them in the next highest grades of the senatorial career. Patricians were allowed to move from the quaestorship to the praetorship without holding any intermediate office.

It is not surprising that ambitious men were disinclined to stand for the once great tribunate which the Emperor's tribunician power completely overshadowed and in which they were no longer able to display their political talents or cultivate popular favor. In 12 B.C. there were so few candidates for the office that a law had to be passed directing the magistrates to draw up a list of knights who possessed the senatorial census of 1,000,000 sesterces. From it, the electorate filled in the vacancies. Any knight who entered the Senate in this manner was given the choice of remaining in it and competing in due time for the higher magistracies or returning to the equestrian order after his tribunate came to an end. When Rome was organized into fourteen wards, or regions, in 7 B.C., certain tribunes selected by lot presided over some of the regions.

The traditional functions of the aediles under the Republic as summarized by Cicero were to supervise the city, the grain supply, and the games. The last two responsibilities were those through which an aedile could win popularity which would further his future career at the polls. When we look at the games and the dole in the following pages, we shall see how these means of currying favor were abolished or greatly reduced, so far as the aediles were concerned. They were left with the supervision of public places, such as markets, baths, taverns, and brothels, with the duty to maintain order and the right to impose fines. Such police activities must have seemed to many to be hardly consistent with senatorial dignity. In fact, in A.D. 6 no one was found willing to stand for the aedileship, and former quaestors and tribunes were compelled to draw lots in order to fill the office.

Although Augustus abolished to a large extent the *raison d'être* of the tribunate and the aedileship by assuming the functions of the former and transferring all or part of the more important functions of the latter to other magistrates or executive officers responsible to himself, he could not do away with the offices themselves. They were hallowed by long existence during the old Republic, and no restored Republic would have been complete without them. But they could also be of use in showing which men were willing to sacrifice their immediate prestige in order to qualify themselves for candidacy to the two highest magistracies, the praetorship and the consulship. Augustus did not wish to see at the top of the government the kind of men who could not put up with a year of relative obscurity or who so lacked faith in themselves that they despaired of being elected to the highest offices unless they were given the means to court the electorate on a large scale with popular legislation and lavish entertainment.

In the later years of the Augustan regime, the usual number of praetors was twelve. Two were charged with the administration of the public treasury, and the rest presided over the permanent courts of justice, or were otherwise concerned with the city's business. But far more important was the fact that with the praetorship a man had politically arrived. He was now eligible to stand for the consulship, the highest office in the state. He was also eligible, before holding the consulship, to serve his country in high posts abroad. He might become governor of one of the minor provinces, either senatorial or imperial. In a senatorial province his title as governor would be proconsul; in an imperial province he was the Emperor's personal representative, his pro-praetorian legate (*legatus Augusti pro praetore*). By law, he could not be selected by lot to govern a senatorial province until five years had elapsed after his city magistracy, but the Emperor could put him at the head of one of his own provinces at any time that suited his pleasure. A former praetor was also qualified to be appointed the commander of a legion.

And then came the consulship, if a former praetor was fortunate enough to reach by ability and favor the peak of the senatorial ladder. We have emphasized the need for former consuls to govern the Empire. The glory rested in the consulate itself. By holding it, a man became identified with Roman history. He joined the line of men by whose names the Roman years were called and took on the aura of an office which symbolized the growth of an insignificant Italian village into the capital of the Mediterranean world. The consul's powers had never been impaired by Augustus. When he was not consul himself, he stood beside the two consuls, completely powerful, but apparently sharing in their work and relieving them of some of their intolerable burdens. Augustus did not intend that the consulship should lose any of its old prestige. When he held it in 5 and 3 B.C., he did so, so that he might introduce his grandsons to public life with the distinction of that office. In these years he could again preside over the Roman Senate by virtue of his election to the highest of the Republican magistracies.

Ten years after holding the consulship, a man might become governor of one of the two great senatorial provinces of Asia or Africa with the title of proconsul. Or, he might be appointed immediately by the Emperor to govern one of the major imperial provinces, where he would be not only the supreme civil administrator but also commander-in-chief of all the armed forces within it. Augustus established both permanent boards and extraordinary commissions to perform specific functions in the administration of the city and the Empire. Consular rank usually entitled a man to sit as chairman of such groups. These posts at home and abroad were the political plums to which an ambitious senator could aspire.

Augustus made a point of treating the Senate with the respect which was due its venerable history. Although "new" men of ability were never excluded from the consulship, the consular lists of the Augustan Age show that Augustus increasingly supported members of families that could boast of a consul among their ascendants.

His relations with the Senate are reflected in the composition of his *consilium,* or formal advisory body. It was entirely composed of senators and included the consuls, fifteen senators chosen by lot, and one member each from the non-consular colleges of magistrates. It assisted Augustus in drawing up the agenda for meetings of the Senate and advised him on matters of policy. So that the maximum number of Senators could enjoy the opportunity of working closely with the Emperor at some time in their career, the membership was changed every six months. Augustus declared publicly the value he placed on the council's deliberations when he stated in one of his edicts that he had taken action on the advice of his senatorial council. But the fact remains that in these matters the final decision belonged to the Emperor, and he was solely responsible for it.

Because of the important part played by the Senate in the administration of Rome and the Empire, the government of Rome under Augustus has been defined as a dyarchy, that is, a rule shared by the Emperor and the Senate, each possessing a circumscribed area of authority and action. In view of what has already been said about the Emperor's actual powers and influence, and the degree of control which he exercised increasingly over the membership of the Senate and the election of magistrates, this definition is not tenable. As the most venerable organ of republican government, the Senate was again made useful and given important functions in the Augustan constitution. It was given a place in the center of the façade of the restored Republic, where it belonged. But if the word partnership implies equality, the Senate was not a true partner, nor even a junior partner, of Augustus in the government. Rather, it was the most important organ of government which the Emperor used in ruling the Roman world with supreme authority through the sum total of the powers which he exercised legally under republican forms.

## The Knights

There were of course many posts in the imperial service which a senator could not be expected to fill because of his high position in the social and political world of Rome. These posts, however, were of more than negligible importance and deserved to be held by freeborn Roman citizens who occupied a place in Roman society which was well above that of the urban plebians. To satisfy this need, Augustus turned to the equestrian order (*ordo equester*), the class of freeborn citizens that stood between the senators and the plebs.

The knights (*equites*) were the big businessmen of Rome. By tradition and law, senators were excluded from participation in trade, banking, and other gainful activities of a financial nature, including the immensely profitable farming of provincial taxes. The senator's income was supposed to come from his land and its products. Although he often found ways through agents and silent partnerships of circumventing tradition and the law, land remained the only large source of wealth which was considered entirely compatible with senatorial status.

Membership in the equestrian order does not seem to have been hereditary. But, naturally, young men who were born into an equestrian family could look forward to being taken into the order more or less as a matter of course. Under Augustus, the future knight had to be born free and descended from a freeborn father and paternal grandfather, possess a fortune of 400,000 sesterces ($20,000), and be of good moral character. His formal enrollment among the knights took place during one of the periodic equestrian censuses, when the Emperor, assisted by a committee of ten senators, revised the lists by adding new members and expelling old ones who had proved themselves unworthy.

The new knight, if he was under the age of thirty-five, was listed among the juniors (*iuniores*) and assigned to one of the cavalry squadrons into which his age group was divided. His horse was provided at public expense for the parade of his group which took place in Rome annually on July 15 under the supervision of senatorial officers. During

Augustus' reign, as many as five thousand knights sometimes participated. This was only a fraction of the entire order, for the men thirty-five and over (the *seniores*) did not take part, and there were many others either on duty abroad or living in Italian provincial towns far from the city who were qualified by age, but prevented from active participation by distance.

The parade was more than a brilliant spectacle in which the younger men could display the solidarity of their order and their equestrian skill. It recalled the past when the knights constituted the cavalry of the Roman army, now largely made up of provincials, and reminded the participants of the duties which they were expected to perform as minor officers in the standing army. What is more, the parade was regularly followed by an inspection or examination of the riders (*equitum probatio*) in which those who failed to make a satisfactory showing could be eliminated from the order. This was no small factor in making the younger knights bear in mind that they were expected to keep themselves in good condition physically as well as mentally and morally and that the honor which had been bestowed could be easily withdrawn. A committee of three senators appointed by Augustus was in charge of the inspection, and we can be sure that the standards by which they judged were fixed by the Emperor himself.

Under Augustus, the military career of the young knight was like that of the young man of senatorial birth who, we recall, was enrolled in the equestrian order until he entered the senate as a quaestor. A knight served in the regular army as the prefect (commander) of an auxiliary unit. Such units were composed of provincials who were not Roman citizens, but who received their citizenship on being honorably discharged after twenty-five years of service. Being either of foot or of horse, they had the paper strength of five hundred or one thousand men. Latin was, of course, the official language of the entire Roman army, and the provincials were compelled to learn it. At the same time, they became familiar not only with Roman discipline and living habits, but also with the high standards of honor, loyalty, and courage which Rome expected all her soldiers to meet. Moreover, a unit was usually assigned to duty on a frontier post which lay at a considerable distance from the place where it had been recruited, and it became customary for the veterans to settle down where they had been discharged and to marry local women with whom they had formed permanent unions and by whom they had often had children. The soldiers were not permitted to marry while in the service, but the imperial government sensibly recognized these liaisons outside the law and legalized them after discharge, with a grant of citizenship to the wife, children, and all future descendants. This policy made a large contribution to the Romanization of the Empire. From a Thracian or Spanish or Gallic tribesman, a man became a Latin-speaking Roman soldier and, later, a Roman citizen at the head of a family of citizens. His ties with the place of his birth had largely been broken, and his chief allegiance would henceforth be to Rome and the Emperor. His sons were qualified to enroll in a legion—legionary soldiers had to be citizens—and, given the normal trend which we find in military families, many a boy seized the opportunity to serve under the eagles that symbolized Rome's military glory.

A young knight might also serve as a tribune (junior officer) in one of the legions. After holding one or a number of these military posts, he could return to private life or be appointed a procurator in one of the imperial provinces. The procurator was the Emperor's financial agent, supervised the collection of taxes, and administered the imperial property. Although he was below the senatorial governor in rank and dignity, he was the Emperor's personal appointee, and a governor would think twice before interfering with him in his field of competence. We know of instances in which there was no love lost between two such men. The Emperor also had financial interests in senatorial provinces, and we find procurators looking after them there.

Another class of procurators was formed by the knights whom Augustus appointed to govern small provinces or administrative districts. They were in fact governors with troops under their command, always auxiliary units or bodies of local militia—except in Egypt, where an equestrian prefect was commander in chief of three legions, each of which had its own equestrian commander. Although Egypt was nominally a province of the Roman people, Augustus treated it, as we have seen, as a private domain over which he exercised complete control. Not only were senators excluded from its administration, but they could not even enter the province without his authorization. To the Egyptians, Augustus was their monarch, and his prefect was their viceroy. The safest kind of viceroy was clearly to be found among able and loyal civil servants whose heads were not likely to be turned by their exalted position. Next to the praetorian prefecture at Rome, the prefecture of Egypt was the highest rung on the equestrian ladder. We shall discuss other important equestrian prefectures when we come to the administration of the city.

### Freemen, Freedmen, and Slaves

In speaking of the senators and knights, we emphasized their political functions under the Augustan constitution.

They were the men who administered the city and the Empire under the Emperor's supervision. At the same time, we had occasion to point out that the role played by the ordinary citizen-voters in elections was finally reduced to a mere formality, although for the sake of tradition Augustus refused to abolish the ghost of this fundamental element in the government of the old Republic.

Something of the same sort can be said about the legislative function of the Roman people. The value which they placed on their exclusive right to make laws is clearly shown by the fact that in 19 B.C. they begged Augustus to make whatever laws he pleased and were willing to swear an oath to obey them. Augustus naturally refused to do so, as contrary to republican tradition. His tribunician power allowed him to bring bills before the people, and the Julian laws which he personally sponsored were undoubtedly passed by the popular assembly. Other magistrates, too, went before the people with bills. Usually they had been drafted in the Senate and if not initiated by the Emperor had at least been approved by him. The *senatus consultum,* or decree of the Senate, did not acquire under Augustus the force of law, as it did later on, but it was used as a convenient vehicle for establishing administrative regulations at home and abroad. The people knew that the matters on which they were called to legislate had Augustus' authority behind them, and they hastened to give them an automatic stamp of approval.

We are speaking now, of course, of Roman citizens who enjoyed full civil rights but were not members of the senatorial or equestrian orders. These citizens, however, were only a part of what we shall call for convenience the common people of Rome. The institution of slavery and the unusual generosity of the Romans in freeing their slaves created a class of men who were free yet did not enjoy all

87

the rights of full Roman citizenship. The freedmen were an important segment of the city's population. Their position in Roman society is inextricably connected with that of the slaves and the freeborn men of the plebian class. We shall treat these component parts of the Roman people together.

During the last centuries of the Republic, when Rome was extending her empire in the East and the West by military conquest, thousands of prisoners of war poured into Rome and Italy as slaves. For example, after the defeat of the Aduatuci, Caesar sold fifty-three thousand Gauls into slavery. The successful campaigns of Augustus and his generals continued to supply the slave markets, but the stream of war captives was beginning to diminish. Slaves could not contract a legitimate marriage, but permanent cohabitation (*contubernium*) was recognized as the servile equivalent of marriage. The children belonged to the master of the parents, and such unions were encouraged for the sake of breeding.

The slaves of ancient Rome were, naturally, of all kinds. Many an educated Greek was forced into servitude by the vicissitudes of war. Such men were naturally in demand in the great households as tutors or to fill posts which required business ability. Livius Andronicus, who founded formal Roman literature by translating Homer's Odyssey into Latin, began his career in Rome as a slave in one of the noble houses. At the other end of the scale were the barbarian captives from the northern provinces, who were relegated to work on the large farms and ranches of the wealthy landowners. They had been the core of the slave rebellion which had darkened the history of the late Republic.

A slave was allowed to accumulate savings (his *peculium*). In the country he might be lent a plot of ground, the produce of which he could sell freely. In the city he might even be set up in business by his master and receive a share of the profits. There were also tips and gifts. A slave's *peculium* belonged legally to his master, but a good master did not lay hands on it. The feeling that his *peculium* was his own encouraged a slave to work industriously to preserve it and increase it, for some day he might be able to use it to purchase his freedom. The master naturally decided whether or not he wished to sell and at what price. He might demand market value, accept a token payment, or make the slave an outright gift of his emancipation.

Vanity, avarice, and expediency, as well as altruism, gratitude, and genuine affection, were all motives for manumission. We know that certain men freed all their slaves by will on their deathbeds so that they might attend the funeral wearing their newly acquired caps of freedom. Others freed their slaves so that they might receive as citizens the periodic gifts which Augustus gave to the Roman people, with the understanding, of course, that they were to share in the largess. A slave could be freed in order to occupy a more responsible position in the same household as a freedman or to serve with greater dignity as his former master's business agent or financial partner. Many a slave owed his manumission to the fact that he had spent years serving his master honestly and loyally. A bond of affection and gratitude between a master and an old nurse or teacher was given concrete expression in the freeing of the latter, and love played its part when a master freed a female slave in order to make her his wife.

There were three forms of formal manumission. One involved the performance of a ceremony before a competent magistrate, usually the praetor at Rome. In another, the slave was added by the censor on the order of his master to the official list of Roman citizens, an obsolete form in the

Augustan Age. In the third, the master gave his slave freedom in his last will and testament. The emancipation naturally did not become effective until the master's death. A master might also direct his heir to free a certain slave. In all these manumissions a tax of five per cent of the slave's value was paid into the treasury.

There was also in the late Republic and early Empire an informal kind of manumission called "among friends" (*inter amicos*). In the presence of friends who served as witnesses the master declared verbally that he gave his slave his freedom. By this act, factual freedom was bestowed on the slave for his lifetime, although in legal theory the freed slave still belonged to his old master. The praetor protected this freedom against any attempt to annul it. But when a freedman of this sort died, he became a slave again so far as his estate was concerned. He could not make a valid will during his lifetime, and his property in its entirety was inherited by his former master who had become his patron. There does not seem to have been any tax on this kind of manumission.

By what seems to have been Augustus' first piece of legislation affecting freedmen, the Emperor rescued those who had been freed informally from the limbo in which they floated between juristic servility and factual freedom. By the *lex Junia* of 17 B.C. the freedom was made complete and irrevocable, and the freedmen were given a firm civil status under Roman law. They obtained Latin rights, which meant that although they were excluded from the franchise and could not stand for Roman magistracies, they possessed the other rights of a Roman citizen, except in regard to the disposition of their property by will. In this matter they remained where they had been before the *lex Junia*: their patrons were the heirs of their entire estates. Finally, the normal tax of five per cent was extended to cover this kind of manumission.

Before we attempt to determine the purpose of this piece of legislation, it will be profitable to glance at other Augustan laws in the same field. We have already mentioned testamentary manumissions. The wealthy man who possessed a large household of slaves had an easy way of acquiring a reputation for gratitude and generosity after death by freeing many or all of his slaves in his will. Since this was a formal kind of manumission, it created large numbers of new citizens indiscriminately. In a household of three hundred slaves, there were bound to be the good, the bad, and the indifferent. Wholesale manumission by will relieved the master of making irksome or invidious choices and had the distinct advantage to him of placing the burden of paying the tax on the heir or heirs.

Augustus curbed the lavishness and irresponsibility of this procedure by means of the *lex Fufia Canina* of 2 B.C. It established a sliding scale of the percentages of slaves who might be freed by will from families of slaves of different sizes. For example, when a family contained thirty to a hundred slaves, only one-fourth could be emancipated; one-fifth was the limit when one hundred to five hundred slaves were involved; and in families of over five hundred, one hundred remained the highest number. This scale protected the interest of the heirs, since they could not be deprived of all the slaves in their inheritance at a single stroke by the testator, who might have been motivated by pure vanity or the desire to make a compensation from beyond the grave for past cruelties or meannesses. It also placed an obligation on the testator to act thoughtfully and to select from among his slaves those who particularly deserved the last and supreme reward within a master's giving.

A master could of course dispose of a slave as he saw fit

regardless of the slave's character. The slave was his property and he could keep, sell, or free him. Augustus was not inclined to interfere with property rights which had been sanctioned by time and tradition. But for the sake of the body politic, he could not allow the worst elements in the servile population to become Roman citizens by formal manumission. The *lex Aelia Sentia* of A.D. 4 did not impair the master's right to free a bad slave in any way he wished, but it created a new class of freedmen into which the slave might enter on receiving his manumission. A slave who had been convicted of a crime or had been severely punished by his master for some transgression entered the class of the *dediticii*. The members of this class possessed the lowest kind of political freedom. They were technically free men but enjoyed none of the rights of the Roman citizen. Augustus wished to rid Rome of these potential troublemakers, and they were compelled to live at least one hundred miles from the city. If they violated this ordinance, their punishment was to be sold back into slavery from which they could never again be emancipated.

Through the same law, Augustus made another attack on rash manumissions. A provision forbade any master under twenty years of age to free a slave unless he had previously been authorized to do so by a committee of five senators and five knights, which had been appointed to examine the reason for the manumission and, presumably, the character of the slave. This prevented young masters from adding to the body of free men unscrupulous slaves who had abused the youth of their masters and drawn them under their influence by shameful means. Loyal service, true gratitude and affection, and increased usefulness in the freed state were all recognized as legitimate causes. Any unworthy relationship was not. Another provision of the law gave to freedmen emancipated before the age of thirty only Latin rights. This tended to make the more responsible slaves wait until that age to buy or request their liberty in order to enter the highest freed status and thus take their positions as new citizens more seriously. It is worth noting that the freedman with Latin rights could acquire full citizenship by marrying a Latin or Roman wife and begetting a child. The founding of a family was interpreted as an indication of responsibility, and the wife, if she was not already a Roman citizen, together with the child were granted full citizenship.

These are the outstanding provisions of the Augustan legislation concerning manumission and the status of freedmen. Its chief purpose, in the eyes of most scholars, was to curb and control the flow of the servile element into the body of Roman citizens. It has even been intimated that if Augustus could have done so, he would have dammed the flow completely, but that tradition and property rights were too strong for him.

This kind of thinking has been greatly influenced by studies which have been made of the national origin of the freedmen and slaves of Rome, based on inscriptions belonging mostly to the first two and one-half centuries of the Empire and found in and around the city. From this evidence one distinguished scholar drew the startling conclusion that during the period just mentioned about ninety per cent of the city's inhabitants were of servile extraction, and, moreover, that the Greek names which predominate in these documents show that the freedman stock, through which this servile blood was poured into the population, was largely composed of Greeks and Hellenized Orientals. Thus a concept arose of the "Orientalization" of Rome during the Empire, and the debasement of the old high Roman moral standards was attributed to this "race mixture."

The value of the statistical evidence itself, its immediate interpretation, and the sweeping conclusion drawn from it have all been widely challenged. Although there can be no doubt that the city offered an excellent market for slaves who possessed the specific skills which the Greeks and Orientals could provide, we lack sufficient evidence to establish an overwhelming preponderance of Eastern freedmen over native freeborn during any circumscribed period of time, especially the Augustan Age. Moreover, it is assumed that the blood of the freeborn possessed a certain Italic purity in Augustan times, an assumption subject to grave doubts.

The Roman campaigns in Asia Minor of the first half of the first century B.C. had flooded Rome with Eastern slaves, and it is only reasonable to believe that many of them, or their children, had already entered into the citizen body through emancipation by the end of the century. Moreover, although in the upper classes there was a strong prejudice against marriages between freeborn and freedmen, whatever legal barrier may once have existed earlier had fallen into obsolescence, and such "mixed" marriages must have taken place frequently between men and women of the same social level. The children of these unions were first and foremost Roman citizens of the plebian class, as were the children of unions between freedmen and freedwomen. There were those undoubtedly in Augustan Rome who taunted them because a parent or both parents had been slaves. The poet Horace, whose father was a freedman, was the target of such shabby jibes, and he answered them with honesty and dignity in a disquisition on a man's true worth. The fact that an ordinary man who had not incited the envy of others had had a freedman grandfather or great-grandfather was probably utterly forgotten.

Augustus was already confronted with an urban plebs,

many of whose members descended from slave stock. He can have had no illusions about this part of the body politic as a stout pillar of Roman greatness and as the custodian of the simple virtues with which its ancestors had defeated Hannibal and the Hellenistic kings. The citizens who wanted to make him dictator or consul for life obviously did not set great store on political independence, provided that they had a patron and a protector. The political degradation of the urban plebs had largely been accomplished in the last decades of the Republic by shameless bribery and a demagogy which descended to the level of political gangsterism. The candidates who brought the votes, the organizers of the political clubs which made a shambles of elections, the wealthy and powerful who surrounded themselves with dependents who supported them politically in return for material favors—the sources of corruption—had not been men in whose veins ran the blood of a Greek or Oriental slave, but members of the senatorial families of Rome.

The damage had been done. Yet the common people had to have a place in the constitution of the restored Republic, regardless of the real position to which they had sunk as a sound or useful political element. We have already seen that Augustus refused to take the election of the higher magistrates formally out of their hands, although he finally controlled it. He could also attempt to improve the character of the urban plebs by making a master exercise choice and judgment in the act of admitting new citizens or potential citizens into the body politic.

For the freedman could be a very useful member of Roman society in its lower levels. His civil status automatically excluded him from the senatorial and equestrian orders and the governmental offices and posts reserved for their members. It also prevented him from serving in the regular army.

His servile origin made it impossible for him to occupy any of the older Roman priesthoods. Thus he turned to the performance of countless other less elevated but highly useful and necessary functions.

We have already said that a slave might be freed so that he could occupy a more responsible position in his master's household. We know of many freedmen who were the administrators of great establishments in which they had once been slaves. The financial responsibilities in such work were not small, and the freedman, while a slave, must have given strong proof of his rectitude and loyalty before receiving his promotion and his freedom. Others of lesser talents or ambition might remain after being emancipated in the same domestic positions as secretaries, butlers, cooks, etc. All these men remained in close contact with their former masters and present patrons. Apart from certain obligations between freedmen and patron which were spelled out by the law, there is ample evidence of bonds of affection and mutual respect. It was not unusual for a Roman to make provision in his family sepulcher for his freedmen and freedwomen.

Many freedmen preferred greater independence. They might be set up in a small business by their patrons or strike out on their own. We find them everywhere throughout the city engaged in trade, industry, commerce, the field of entertainment, and the professions. Those who had been slaves had not inherited the Roman's scorn for manual labor and business, and they brought to their activities ambition, intelligence, and skill. They did not consider it more honorable to live miserably on the dole or as a hanger-on of some great man than to earn their own livings. They knew well that money was their best friend, and they took its acquisition seriously. They were willing to start at the bottom and work to the top and to pursue callings which even the poorest freeborn Roman would have considered degrading. Some naturally remained economically where they had started, and their descendants melted into the great amorphous mass of the common people. Others acquired wealth which enabled their sons and grandsons to climb higher on the social and political ladder. Finally, even under Augustus, freedmen were not entirely excluded from participation in the administration of the Empire. The secretarial staff which attended to the Emperor's paper work was composed of his own freedmen and slaves. This staff was the beginning of the great imperial bureaus, the freedmen chiefs of which were to become some of the most powerful men in Rome under later Emperors. Augustus kept them well in hand.

Freedmen of good character, then, could bring new vigor and a spirit of enterprise into the urban plebs. Augustus was naturally interested in seeing that this part of the body politic was not swollen with undesirable, or even criminal, elements through large-scale indiscriminate manumissions. But there is no reason to believe that he did not welcome the addition of decent, industrious freedmen to the citizen body, regardless of their national origin as slaves. The hypothesis that he was attempting to avoid or slow down "racial mixture" is belied by the liberality of his own marriage laws. There was no ban which kept a freedman from marrying any freeborn person, except one from the senatorial order. The high aristocracy who had the task of governing Rome and her empire, and enjoyed the privileges which went with it, had to be a caste apart from the rest of the population.

In speaking of the freedmen among the common people, we have also been speaking of the freeborn, for the children of freedmen were exactly that. In the Italic towns there were undoubtedly simple men and women who could boast of never having had a slave ancestor. In Rome, conditions which we have mentioned militated against this situation. In guilds and burial clubs we find freedmen and freemen side by side, and the freemen may have had fathers or grandfathers who had been slaves. We can picture the common people of Rome as a large stream of freeborn men which was constantly being increased from a tributary of former slaves, the waters of which as they entered the main stream were soon reduced to the same consistency.

Among the common people of Rome there were undoubtedly many freeborn men who were honest in their individual relations and did their share in doing the city's hard and humble work. These men together with the freedmen built the buildings, tended the shops, and produced the necessities and luxuries which the city needed. There were others who were good-for-nothings by character or choice and preferred a half-starved idleness to standing on their own feet. In the pages of the historians all these people, good and bad, appear only as a political group, and it is precisely in this role that they show us their worst side: the side which had been infected by the greed and venality of the upper classes during the late Republic.

Augustus did not have the slightest intention of creating a democracy in the modern sense of the word or of running the Empire through a representative government. The towns and cities of Italy and the Empire had their municipal governments to look after local affairs, and through provincial councils and other devices larger territorial units were given some limited powers. But the Empire was governed from Rome by the Emperor with the help of an elite who belonged within the system of the old city-state. He had made them an indispensable part of his new order. The government of the city and the Empire by the Emperor and this group was in fact complete.

When the people showed indifference to their chief responsibility, the election of magistrates, or handled it badly by clamoring for a dictator or rioting at the polls, they were an obstacle to, not a functioning part of, the kind of regime which Augustus wished to establish. Increasingly, then, they were relegated to an impotent position in the façade of the restored Republic. The fault lay with historical circumstances. Augustus could not bring to life again a spirit and discipline which had long been dead, nor could he sacrifice good government to tradition.

# IV

# THE CITY

WHEN THE EMPEROR CONSTANTIUS visited Rome for the first time in A.D. 357, he was dazzled by the ancient city's magnificence. The historian Ammianus Marcellinus, who gives us an account of the visit, mentions specifically, and sometimes with a descriptive detail, some of the buildings which particularly impressed him. He lists the public baths, "as large as provinces," the solid mass of the Amphitheater, "to whose summit human vision climbs with difficulty," the Pantheon, "like a circular part of a city, covered by a high and beautiful vault," the lofty columns carrying the statues of earlier emperors, the Temple of the City, the Forum of Peace, the Theater of Pompey, the Odeum, and the Stadium. Above all, the Forum of Trajan filled the Emperor with awe and admiration.

Of course, Constantius saw the city at its architectural peak. Nevertheless, the visitor today who is willing to view the remains of ancient Rome with more than cursory attention will understand the Emperor's feelings. For he will be walking in the Emperor's footsteps and gazing on some of the buildings at which he marveled. A few, like the Pantheon and the Columns of Trajan and Marcus Aurelius are virtually intact; some, like the Colosseum and the Baths of Caracalla and Diocletian, are partly ruined; still others, like the Theater of Pompey or the Stadium of Domitian have left few traces on the surface of modern Rome except in the configuration of the city's topography. (The Piazza Navona, for example, follows the lines of Domitian's Stadium.) On bringing them together in his mind, he may well conclude that at one place and one period men never built more skillfully and lavishly in the grandiose manner.

The fallacy here would lie in the concept of one period. For the period would be that of ancient Rome, and, as we have already seen, ancient Rome lasted some twelve hundred years. In the course of so many centuries, there was constant building, destruction, and rebuilding, and fundamental changes took place in architecture and methods of construction. It is a long way from the rude huts on the Palatine to the Rome of Constantius. The city of Augustus is somewhat nearer the latter in time, but it must not be mistaken for the city which Constantius saw. As the Augustan constitution marked a new political era which divided the old Republic from the new Empire, so did the city of Rome enter a new and imperial phase in the Augustan Age. The building program of Augustus began the trend which culminated in the city of Constantius. But it must be kept in mind that it was only a beginning.

To illustrate, of the buildings mentioned by Ammianus in his description of Constantius' visit only the following could have been seen by a person of the Augustan Age: the Theatre of Pompey (dedicated in 55 B.C.) and the Baths of Agrippa (if Ammianus was not thinking solely of the far greater baths of later times). Other buildings too, which compel the modern visitor's admiration, are post-Augustan. For example, the Arches of Titus, Septimius Severus, and Constantine, the palaces on the Palatine, the Temple of Antoninus and Faustina and the Basilica of Maxentius. In fact, if by some singular twist of fate, we had no remains of ancient Rome later than the Augustan Age, it can be said confidently that the ruins of Rome would never have cast so strong a spell on the creative imaginations of the countless writers and artists who have made them one of the most fascinating themes in the repertory of Western literature and art.

Of a city which interests us at a definite period of time in its past history, we are likely to ask first, "How big was it then?" By this bigness we usually mean the size of the population. Unfortunately, in regard to Augustan Rome we are confronted with an irremediable lack of vital statistics. We simply do not have anything corresponding to our census reports of today. We know that 320,000 members of the urban plebs received gifts of money from Augustus in 5 B.C. and that about 200,000 were on the dole three years later. These are our firmest figures. But they do not permit us to estimate, even approximately, the size of the plebian class as a whole because the distributions were made to adult male citizens, with the possible exception in the case of the dole of some widows and orphans. We do not know how many of the men were supporting families, or the size of an average plebian family. Furthermore, there were slaves and foreigners who inhabited the city without being citizens. As for the two upper classes, we know that 600 men sat in the Senate and about 5,000 were on the equestrian rolls. Again there is no way of estimating the number of their dependents.

We have suggested above that no precise figure exists for the number of slaves in Augustan Rome. This is an obstinate fact. It is worth noting how some scholars have valiantly attempted to get around it, for it furnishes the clearest illustration of the fallacies involved in reaching an untenable solution to a problem which cannot be solved for lack of firm and pertinent evidence.

The historian Tacitus tells us that Senator Pedanius Secundus possessed four hundred slaves at the time of his death in A.D. 61. Let us accept this number as exact or approximately so. First, we must ask whether so large a household was in any way typical of those maintained by the noble and wealthy of the Augustan Age. We know of senators of relatively modest means. Within the order, how many could have supported so extravagant a retinue, and among those who could, how many would have cared to do so? We do not know.

We have scattered notices of more humble men who were masters of from one to twenty slaves. These people appear accidentally in our sources, and although we sometimes know the different degrees of wealth which they represent, we do not know what proportions of society as a whole their financial classes constituted. Nor do we know whether the number of their slaves was large or small in relation to their means and social position. Such inconclusive data certainly do not permit us to assume that the average number of slaves in the household of an ordinary citizen was ten.

Again, a famous passage in Galen informs us that in Pergamum, in Asia Minor, there was about one slave to every two free persons in the second century A.D. (He gives the total population of the town, probably excluding the children, as 120,000). This is indeed welcome evidence, so far as Pergamum is concerned. But have we any right to remove it from its relatively small provincial setting in order to apply it to the metropolis of the Empire into which thousands of captives seized in the course of Rome's conquest in all parts of the Mediterranean world had been poured? Moreover, what good is Galen's equation to us, since we lack an indispensable part of it—the number of free men and women in Rome's population? Yet, on the basis of such scattered notices, reinforced with speculations on the number of public slaves in industry and elsewhere, we are told that the servile population of Rome numbered 380,500 or 200,000 or 127,000.

Other approaches have been used which have proved equally treacherous. For example, the size of the population has been worked out on the basis of the amount of grain imported annually from overseas. Here the amount is calculated on a combination of figures, one of which belongs to a period some sixty years after the Augustan Age. The other indispensable factor in this approach is a knowledge of the average consumption per capita. This we do not have.

Then, there has been the archaeological approach. It consists in attempting to determine the area within the Aurelian walls (begun about A.D. 272) which was occupied by such things as temples, public buildings, squares, and streets and was thus exempt from human habitation. The inhabited area is then attained by simple subtraction. But here also there are insuperable obstacles. Most of ancient Rome is still buried under the modern city, and conjectures about the sizes of buildings, streets, and squares, of which little or no traces remain, vary to a fantastic degree. In estimating areas which can be partially or totally measured, two experts in that field of Roman topography differ by more than one million square meters. When their conjectures about the size of the unmeasurable areas are added, the difference increases to over two million.

To whatever size is obtained for the habitable area, an average density of population is then applied. Since we do not have the slightest idea of the density of population in

Rome at any time during her ancient period, we must have recourse to the statistics furnished by modern cities. This is a hazardous procedure in itself and becomes even more so when the next inescapable step is taken, namely, choosing a certain period in the life of a modern city and applying that population density to ancient Rome. For the population density of a modern city changes from census to census and does not stand in constant ratio to the city's growth in area. Even if we knew precisely the size of the inhabited area of Augustan Rome, and we do not, it would be a pure piece of good luck if one of the many population densities, of modern Rome for example, was chosen which was even approximately applicable to the ancient city.

With calculations of this sort there is often combined an estimate of population by private houses (*domus*) and by apartment houses (*insulae*). Two documents which we call *Regionaries* have come down to us from antiquity listing the buildings, public facilities, and landmarks of each of the fourteen "regions" (wards) of the city at the end of the third and the beginning of the fourth centuries A.D. A summary of each document informs us that there were 46,-602 apartment houses and 1790 private houses in Rome at this time. An average number of inhabitants has been assigned to each unit of both kinds of dwellings. But even if each unit within its kind had been built to the same specifications, which of course was as impossible then as it is today, and we knew the exact size of each, we could not tell how densely each was inhabited. Finally, we may ask one more unanswerable question: to what extent is it permissible to transfer the figures given for these dwellings to a period some three hundred years earlier?

The reader must therefore beware of figures reached by any of these methods, used separately or in conjunction with each other. Rome in the Augustan Age was considered a large city by those who knew it. With prosperity, the expansion of the imperial bureaucracy, and the attractions of a metropolis, it probably continued to enlarge its population during the period. But to say that it was inhabited by one million people means no more than that one million seems a comfortable round figure, big enough to be properly imperial and small enough not to be outrageous. If it is right, it is no more than a lucky guess. Smaller or larger numbers may be nearer the truth.

When an Augustan Roman spoke of the Seven Hills of Rome, he was thinking of the seven hills on the left bank of the Tiber. Four were isolated—the Capitoline, Palatine, Aventine and Caelian. Two, the Quirinal and Viminal, jutted out as promontories from the tableland to the north, which was called the Esquiline and counted as a separate hill. The number seven was canonical, and when other hills such as the Vatican and the Janiculum appear in later official lists, they are substituted for some of the original seven.

The hills on the left bank were created in geologic times by erosion. Water pouring down on the Latin plain from the surrounding mountains formed streams which ate into the loose tufa at points of least resistance before emptying into the river which became the historical Tiber. In some places the force was sufficient to cut off parts of the tableland completely, forming masses of isolated terrain such as the Palatine hill. In others the water carved out valleys within the tableland proper, such as the one which divides the Quirinal from the Viminal.

Constant leveling, building, and rebuilding throughout Rome's long existence has tended to blunt the outlines of the city's hills. From the Pincio one can still see clearly the ridges across the Tiber which stretch from Monte Mario,

in the north, southward to Monte Verde. Capitoline, Palatine, and Aventine still stand out clearly. But the visitor can
approach some of the other hills in the northern part of the
modern city by gentle slopes which betray no distinctive
changes in the terrain.

The earliest settlements in the area of the later city were
all on hills, the steep or precipitous sides of which afforded
natural protection. We can assume that in places where a
hill was easily accessible over level ground, as was true of
the Quirinal, for example, where it joined the tableland to
the north, an artificial barrier was erected. It probably consisted of an earth wall with a ditch on its outer side. There
is no reason to believe that any unbroken line of fortification
bound together these early settlements. They were separate
communities, each attending to its own protection. Moreover, the valleys between the hills were uninhabited, and
it would have been pointless to defend them.

The earliest evidence for a more comprehensive system
of defense is furnished by the remains of an agger, a defen-
sive mound of earth, which was built across the level land
to the northeast of the Quirinal, Viminal, Cispius, and Op-
pius Hills. It can be dated at the end of the sixth or the beginning of the fifth centuries. There can be no doubt that it
is the famous agger which is attributed to King Servius Tullius in our literary sources. It was meant to protect the city,
in which the separate settlements had long been united, on
the side that was devoid of any natural defenses. It is not
known whether walls giving the city a continuous line of
fortification were constructed across the valleys that divided
the other hills at this time. The evidence so far is inconclusive and can be interpreted in different ways.

What is certain is that Gallic invaders captured the city
easily, with the exception of the Capitoline, in or about 387

B.C., after defeating the Roman army in the field. It is clear from our ancient accounts that the Capitoline was then serving as the arx, or fortified stronghold, where the inhabitants could take refuge when compelled to abandon the rest of the city. The Gallic catastrophe taught the Romans a bitter lesson. It made them realize the need for a continuous line of strong fortifications surrounding all parts of the city. In 378, a massive wall began to be raised composed of blocks of Grotta Oscura tufa. On the side protected by the Servian agger, the new wall was built against it on the outside. In other places it swung far out beyond the line which earlier fortifications could be reasonably assumed to have taken, if they actually existed. Now all the hills and valleys of Rome on the left bank of the Tiber were protected.

The Romans of the Augustan Age identified the wall of 378 with the fortifications of King Servius Tullius. Later generations quite naturally accepted the identification and it is only relatively recently that archaeologists have made the necessary correction. The imposing stretch of blocks near the Termini Station survive from the wall of the fourth century B.C.

The historian Dionysius of Halicarnassus, who wrote in Rome during the Augustan Age, tells us that the city wall was difficult to find because of the buildings which had encroached upon it from all sides. The fact is that the city had now outgrown its republican wall in two ways. First, the area of continuous habitation which determined the actual size of the city extended beyond the old mural circuit in many directions. Secondly, and this is far more important, Rome no longer needed this kind of protection. The last large scale restoration of the wall of which we know took place in 87 B.C. and was caused by the Roman forces of Marius who were attempting to seize the city in a civil war. The last foreign enemy who had been seen at the gates of Rome was Hannibal in 211 B.C. A personal inspection of the defenses convinced him that Rome could hold out indefinitely against any siege or assault which he was capable of undertaking. In the Augustan Age the city was protected by the frontiers of the Empire in distant provinces and by the sea which Rome had made her own.

Horace, who took pleasure in strolling about the city, tells us in one of his *Satires* what had happened to the Servian agger near the Esquiline Gate in the Augustan Age. During the Republic an area on the outer side of the mound and wall at this point had been made into a miserable burial ground for slaves and paupers. The wealthy Maecenas had acquired this land and turned it into part of the pleasure gardens which he laid out on both sides of the agger. The latter was allowed to remain as a sunny promenade from which a view of the gardens could be enjoyed from above. Most of the old gates continued to exist as decorative landmarks. We are reminded of the boulevards of Paris, large parts of which are located on the line of earlier fortifications. The relationship is preserved in the word "boulevard" which originally meant "bulwark."

Rome, though virtually unfortified, was not unarmed. The presence of troops in Rome during the restored Republic was a startling innovation. It was a fundamental principle of the old Republic that the city should have no permanent garrison. Troops were raised in the city to fight in the field. A general, as we have seen, was forced to lay down his imperium on crossing Rome's sacred boundaries except on the day of his triumph, and it was on that day alone that his army could enter the city with him. It was perhaps the most monarchic act which Augustus performed when he stationed regular military units in Rome.

109

# ROME

During the civil wars which preceded Augustus' victory at Actium and the beginning of the Augustan peace, a new kind of military unit emerged. It was the cohort, composed of chosen soldiers or veterans who stood in a particularly close relation to their commander, guarding his person and accompanying him into battle. Augustus discharged a certain number of his praetorian cohorts after Actium, but kept nine of them on active duty. They were presumably under his direct command, since we do not hear of the appointment of praetorian prefects until 2 B.C.

In Rome, the praetorian cohorts were definitely the Emperor's troops, but not his bodyguard. A group of German slaves assured the safety of the Emperor's person. Augustus had to disband them in A.D. 9 in deference to the hatred toward them which swept the people after the terrible defeat inflicted by the Germans on Quintilius Varus and his legions. Augustus must have felt that it was less invidious to use foreign slaves in this capacity than freeborn Romans who were members of the regular army. He never mentions the praetorians in the *Res Gestae* and, as we shall see shortly, made their presence in Rome as inconspicuous as possible. But he must have felt that the need for a trained military elite whose devotion to himself was beyond suspicion outweighed in importance the rupture with republican tradition. In case of outright rebellion in the city against his regime or of sedition in the provinces involving other military units, Augustus had at hand the necessary force to take vigorous countermeasures.

Neither rebellion nor sedition took place. Conspiracies against the Emperor's life were the work of small groups of individuals. When we think of the praetorians in their later notorious role as emperor-makers and the lurid scenes in which they were destined to participate, we are amazed at

110

their docility and obscurity in the Augustan Age. They were in and about Rome as a precautionary measure. Augustus saw to it that they did not overstep the limits of the functions he had assigned to them.

Each of the nine cohorts was commanded by a tribune (not to be confused with a political tribune). We are not sure whether its strength under Augustus was one thousand or five hundred men. (It was certainly one thousand in later times.) The cohort was divided into six centuries of infantry and had a complement of cavalry. The original soldiers were veterans of Augustus' civil wars. As vacancies occurred, they were filled with men who came from parts of Italy which had long been Romanized. The Praetorian Guard was a privileged corps in pay, length of service, and many other ways. It was open exclusively to Roman citizens who had maintained the manly qualities of their ancestors in the Italic towns. The Roman plebians of the city of Rome were notably absent from among the praetorians.

We may now ask what Augustus did to make the untraditional and unconstitutional presence of troops within the city more palatable to the Roman people. First, he never allowed more than three cohorts to be within the city at the same time. The others were stationed in summer and winter camps in neighboring towns. Moreover, the soldiers in the city had no permanent camp. The *castra praetoria,* imposing remains of which can be seen today built into the Aurelian walls near the Porta Nomentana, was not built until A.D. 23, under Tiberius, Augustus' successor. The Augustan praetorians were scattered in billets throughout the city and were probably dressed as civilians. They must, of course, have had a headquarters where they received orders, but we do not know where or of what kind. It is noteworthy that when Augustus finally appointed a high command, he appointed two commanders, something of an absurdity in a military unit, yet reflecting, where it did not belong, the old republican principle of collegiality.

The large scale disorders which were common features of the political life of the late Republic had shown only too clearly that Rome did not have an adequate police force. Minor magistrates, the *tresviri capitales,* with a force of public slaves, had proved themselves incapable of handling the political gangs which turned elections and other legitimate activities of the assemblies into scenes of riot and bloodshed. The *tresviri* had the authority of the higher magistrates behind them and acted under their orders. But this very fact often impeded any effective action, since there were often those in the highest places who tolerated or even promoted the most vicious assaults on public safety, provided that their own political ends were furthered by them. Perhaps the most terrifying example of the anarchy which could prevail in Rome occurred in 52 B.C. The followers of the former tribune Publius Clodius, enraged by his assassination at the hands of a political rival, erected a makeshift funeral pyre in the middle of the Senate house with which they managed to cremate the corpse of their hero and burn down the building at one stroke. Three of the tribunes of that year incited the mob to this act of violence.

Augustus did not intend that Rome should be disfigured by any such shameless incidents during his regime. But the solution of the problem of maintaining public order could not lie in backing up the *tresviri* with greater vigor and placing more public slaves under their command. They could be left the minor tasks of apprehending and punishing petty criminals and runaway slaves. Any large scale riots would be largely the work of Roman citizens, and armed slaves should not be sent against them. Trained and disciplined soldiers were the only answer. They alone could be trusted to obey orders scrupulously, to keep their heads in precarious situations, and to command respect from those whom they were restraining. Their presence alone in Rome would have a salutary effect.

It was clearly undesirable that the Emperor's own praetorians should perform the duties of a riot police. They were the elite corps of the whole Roman army and had not been chosen to disperse mobs. Then, too, the praetorians were closely connected with Augustus in fact and in men's minds. Whatever odium they incurred in the performance of police duties was bound to fall in some measure on the Emperor himself. But this would also be true of other troops which might be raised for the specific purpose of policing the capital, if they remained under Augustus' direct command. The Emperor would always have the final word. But there should be some respected and highly placed individual who could give the immediate orders and take the responsibility for them. Furthermore, it could not be one of the regular magistrates, who held their office annually and were occupied with other business. A new office was needed in which a man could remain for an indefinite number of years and devote himself exclusively to maintaining law and order in the city.

Augustus found a typical solution: to revive an old republican office and give it new functions. Under the early Republic it had been customary for the consuls, when both had to be absent from the city, to appoint a city prefect (*praefectus urbi*) to conduct legal business and to supervise the city's administration in general. The creation in the fourth century B.C. of an urban praetor who was the repre-

113

sentative of the consuls in their absence and bound legally to remain in the city made the urban prefecture superfluous. It fell quickly into abeyance.

Augustus revived the office on the occasion of his first absence from Rome (26 B.C.) after the restoration of the Republic. This was the somewhat tenuous link with the original function of the urban prefecture, for Augustus was consul at the time. The man he chose to fill the prefecture was Marcus Valerius Messala, a former consul who belonged to one of the oldest and greatest families in Rome. He had fought on the side of Brutus and Cassius at Philippi, but later became one of Augustus' loyal supporters and commanded the center of his fleet at Actium. He continued to serve the Emperor and his country with ability and devotion, but kept his dignity and his freedom of judgment and action. He was one of the members of the old guard who saw Rome's salvation in the new order and was willing to contribute his part in making it work. But he wanted it to work as far as possible along traditional lines. He accepted the urban prefecture, but laid it down after a few days. His alleged reason was that he did not know how to conduct the office. The fact was that his republican conscience was troubled.

The troops which Augustus placed under the command of Messala were three urban cohorts (*cohortes urbanae*). We do not know whether they were raised at this time from soldiers picked from other units or had been formed earlier. The fact that they were numbered X through XII, thus continuing the numbers of the praetorian cohorts, I through IX, could indicate that all of them were formed at the same time. It would have been quite natural for Augustus first to provide the force and then to solve the problem of its command.

According to Tacitus, their principal duty under Augustus was to keep order among the slaves and the citizens who would dare to be unruly and were not afraid of force. Each urban cohort was organized as a regular military unit under the command of a tribune. When the praetorian camp was built in A.D. 23, they shared its facilities with the praetorians. But in pay, length of service, and bonuses and gifts, they occupied an inferior position to the imperial elite. The promotions among the units of the city garrison were from the urban to the praetorian cohorts.

When Messala laid down the office in 26, Augustus may have waited to fill it again out of deference to the aversion of the old guard represented by Messala. But he was still convinced of the desirability of his original plan regarding the command. He soon found another man of consular rank, Statilius Taurus, who did not share Messala's scruples. By the end of the Augustan regime the city prefect, as police commissioner of Rome, was a regular part of the city's administrative machinery.

In republican Rome the prevention and extinction of fires had been a sorry business. The *tresviri,* whom we have just mentioned in connection with public safety, assisted by their band of public slaves, were the city's only public fire department. They were helped from time to time by the aediles and tribunes. The system was inadequate, and devastating fires became common occurrences. As always, there were some who knew how to profit from the disasters. When a fire broke out, Marcus Licinius Crassus would rush to the scene and, while the fire was still burning, would offer a ridiculously low sum for the property and the neighboring buildings which were in danger of being engulfed by the flames. He kept a special band of five hundred slaves who had been trained as construction workers. On the site of the ruins he had them build houses or apartments which brought in a handsome revenue. This was one of the ways through which he acquired large parts of the city's real estate and thus became the richest man of the late Republic.

Augustus could not tolerate this state of affairs. It was hardly worth while to embellish a city of which parts would be constantly gutted and disfigured by fire. His first step, however, was taken with due regard for republican tradition. The general supervision of the city (the *cura urbis*) had been since early times the province of the aediles. Moved to action by a fire which took place in 23 B.C., Augustus gave these magistrates a band of six hundred slaves for the specific purpose of fighting fires. The measure was inadequate. We have already mentioned the aedile who successfully courted popular favor during Augustus' absence from Rome (22–19 B.C.) by organizing his own slaves into a fire company and putting out fires at his own expense.

After the reorganization of the city in 7 B.C. into 14 wards (*regiones*) and some 265 precincts (*vici*), a new system was tried. The firemen-slaves who had served the aediles were now placed under the orders of the precinct leaders. This arrangement proved to be no more satisfactory than the one which preceded it. After a bad fire in A.D. 6, Augustus took the last inevitable step.

He set up a corps of professional firemen who were called *vigiles* (watchmen). They were organized into seven cohorts, each of which had a strength of one thousand men and was commanded by a tribune. The commander in chief was a prefect of equestrian rank, the *praefectus vigilium,* who was directly responsible to the Emperor.

Although their cohorts were organized along military lines, a fundamental difference distinguished the watchmen from the urban soldiers and the praetorians. Whereas the latter had to be freeborn Roman citizens, membership in

116

the corps of *vigiles* was restricted to freedmen. They were probably given Latin rights on enrollment, but even so they were a full grade below the others in civil status. Their functions, which had previously been performed by slaves, had something menial about them, and we can readily understand Augustus' reluctance to impose them on freeborn Roman soldiers. On the other hand, by choosing freedmen, the danger was avoided of organizing seven thousand slaves into military formations in which they would acquire the training and feeling of solidarity which might well be a source of danger in uneasy times.

The division of the city into fourteen wards clearly determined the organization of the corps of watchmen. Each cohort was made responsible for the control of fires in two adjacent regions and had its headquarters at a place from which both could be conveniently supervised. We hear later of posts or subheadquarters in each region, and they may have been part of the original Augustan system. In addition to their chief duties as firemen, the watchmen exercised certain police functions which belonged naturally to their nightly rounds. They had the right to arrest thieves and housebreakers, and their prefect sat in judgment on them. The prefect could also reprimand or punish with a cudgeling persons who had shown criminal negligence in handling fire. It was his duty to warn all tenants that they must keep water in their apartments in the event of an outbreak.

In the urban cohorts and the watchmen, Augustus gave Rome two organizations which were long overdue. There was now a police force in existence which was capable of preventing or quelling any large-scale disorders. The way had been made harder for the ordinary criminal, and fire fighting was in the hands of a disciplined and well-equipped force. There would still be riots, crimes, and fires, but Au-

117

gustus had at least taken the first comprehensive measures to make his capital a safer place in which to live.

We have said above that the organization of the city determined the kind of organization given to the corps of watchmen. It was in 7 B.C. that Augustus divided the city into fourteen regions or wards. The city limits were not made to coincide artificially with any previous line of demarcation such as the old Servian wall or the pomerium, the city's sacred boundary, but were considered to stand wherever continuous building came to an end. Thus, as the city expanded into the surrounding country, the city limits moved out with it, and the regions on the periphery increased in size. Under Augustus the wards seem to have been known by their numbers alone, but in time popular usage gave them the name of some conspicuous landmark or identified them with their geographic location. For example, Regions IX and XI came to be called "Circus Flaminius" and "Circus Maximus" respectively; Regions XIII and XIV, "Aventine" and "Across the Tiber" (*trans Tiberem,* the modern Trastevere). From the aediles, tribunes, and praetors an administrative head for each region was annually chosen by lot.

Each region in turn was divided into a number of smaller units called *vici,* or precincts. The word *vicus,* when applied to a city, meant both a street and the section of the city lying in its vicinity. In the time of the Emperor Vespasian (A.D. 69–79) there were 265 *vici* in Rome, and probably the number was not very much smaller under Augustus. Each *vicus* had four masters (*magistri*) who were elected annually by inhabitants of the section from among the freedmen. They had slave assistants (*ministri*). Their function was chiefly religious in that they attended to the cult of the protecting deities of the crossroads (the *lares compitales*), whose festivals were celebrated in the spring and summer. The Genius of Augustus was added to this cult. In the Italic tradition, a man's genius, in the narrowest sense, was his reproductive power or virility; in the widest, the sum total of his vitality. It was quasi divine, for a libation was made to it on a man's birthday; yet it vanished with the same man's death. The genius of the head of a family, the *pater familias,* was particularly respected by members of his household.

When the Genius of Augustus was included in the sacrifices to the lares of a *vicus,* it did not mean that the Emperor had laid claim to divine status or that this status had been imposed upon him. In fact, Augustus made every effort to prevent a religious cult of his person from growing up in Italy. But this he could not successfully accomplish. Too many in Rome's cosmopolitan population were used to the Hellenistic worship of monarchs as revealed divinities and sensed the divine element in the Emperor's person and benefactions. The cult of his genius, which had nothing in it to offend the most stubborn Roman traditionalist, would allow those who wished to worship Augustus as divine to do so. Others could see in the ceremonies at the crossroads nothing more than symbols of loyalty and affection paid to a mortal father and generous protector.

There is an interesting passage at the end of the Fifth Book of Livy which throws some light on the appearance of Augustan Rome. After the sack of Rome by the Gauls in 390 B.C., according to Livy's chronology, the tribunes urged the plebians to abandon their ruined city and emigrate to Veii, an Etruscan town which had recently been captured by the Romans in a virtually undamaged state. Owing largely to the eloquent resistance of Camillus, the tribune's bill was not passed, and the Romans began to rebuild their city. Tiles were furnished at public expense, and everyone was permitted to lay hands on whatever building material he could find, provided that he gave surety that his building would be finished within a year. The speed with which the reconstruction was carried on prevented the laying out of straight streets, and men built indiscriminately on their own or another's property wherever they found a vacant space. "This is the reason," Livy says in terminating this passage, "that the old sewers which were originally laid down in public property now pass here and there under private houses and the [present] form of the city resembles more a squatters' settlement than a planned community."

It is quite clear that Livy, who was writing this part of his *History* around 27 B.C., was using the aftermath of the Gallic occupation to explain and excuse the lack of any plan or system in the streets of Rome of his day. The fact was, however, that no foreign enemy was needed to turn Rome into a labyrinth. Rome, like ancient Athens, grew up in a haphazard fashion, and the terrain, man's convenience, and subsequent habit established the footpaths and trails which later became streets. This lack of pattern was too firmly fixed to be changed when the Romans became acquainted with the city planning developed by the Greeks. Even after the building program of Augustus, the residential parts of Rome were very little changed. Tacitus has given us a fine description of the city before large parts of it were destroyed under Nero by the fire of A.D. 64. In it he mentions the twisting streets, the huge and shapeless blocks of houses, and the tall buildings of "Old Rome." Nero rebuilt the destroyed areas in the modern style with orderly blocks, wide streets, and broad squares and porticoes. There were those who deplored the access of sunshine which the new architecture permitted and yearned for the healthier days when the streets were plunged in gloom.

The buildings which lined these streets were of course of

various kinds. But if we put aside for the moment temples and other public monuments, we can isolate certain common types of construction: the private house (*domus*), the apartment house or tenement (*insula*), and the shop (*taberna*).

The private houses of Pompeii probably give us a fair idea of the kind of house which the well-to-do person of the upper classes inhabited in Augustan Rome. Many of these Roman houses had already been in existence for some time. Augustus himself, who made a point of living modestly, occupied a house on the Palatine which he had acquired from the family of the orator Hortensius. It was conspicuous for its short porticoes built of local stone and its lack of marble adornment and elaborate floors.

These houses, old or new, were built around a central room open to the sky which was called the atrium. A vestibule led into it from the street. Behind the atrium there might be a courtyard surrounded by a portico (the peristyle), or a garden, or both. Smaller rooms were located on the long sides. This typical arrangement was subject to many variations according to the wealth and taste of the owner and the size and shape of the area on which the house was built. We can see the variations in the houses of Pompeii and must assume that they were even more striking in the capital, where land was at a premium and became increasingly valuable as more space was required to put into effect the imperial building program.

In even the most beautiful and elaborate houses the bedrooms were likely to be mean. They served purely as a place to sleep. The atrium was the business office of the head of the family. It was there that he received his freedmen and clients, gave advice, conducted financial transactions, and kept his strongbox and accounts. The masks of his ancestors

121

affixed to the walls of the atrium constantly reminded him of his social and political position, his privileges and obligations. We shall return to the masks again.

Family life was centered in the peristyle. This amounted to living out of doors in spring, summer, and autumn. The portico afforded shade from the sun and shelter from the spring and autumn rains. The center was laid out as a formal garden with statues and fountains. It was an island of quiet in the midst of a noisy and bustling city.

The walls of the rooms were decorated with frescoes. In the Augustan Age, what we call the second Pompeian style prevailed. It was an architectural style which went beyond the sole function of colorful adornment. The eye was confronted by a wall which was painted to represent the façade of a building with columns, pilasters, cornices, porticoes, friezes, statues, or whatever else occurred to the painter. Although the building was a product of his imagination, the proportions were those of real architecture. Furthermore, by a skillfull use of perspective, the eye was drawn through the openings in the façade to a second or third plane. It looked through a doorway or window onto other buildings or out to a landscape. Or a mythological scene was framed like a painting between architectural elements of the first plane. The whole gave an illusion of depth and added fictitiously to the size of the room. Vistas had been created which were impossible to obtain in a crowded city, and the Roman genius for architecture and love for the structural were playing a new and charming role in a different medium.

One of the most agreeable events of Rome today is dining out of doors during the many months when the weather itself is an invitation to this way of eating. In the larger houses of Pompeii we often find two dining rooms, for winter and for summer. The latter was built in a garden or in some other place where the air was freshest. By the Augustan Age, the custom of reclining on couches placed around a table at formal dinners was widespread among the upper classes. In many dining rooms (*triclinia*) the couches were built into the room. The usual arrangement was three couches, each having space for three people, on three sides of the table. Hence the formal dinner party was limited to nine, the number of Muses.

The atrium house had a long history in Rome. It belonged to the agricultural tradition of the old Italic life. Cato the Censor had to buy and tear down two of them in 184 B.C. when he built Rome's first basilica at the edge of the Forum. The house of Publius Africanus was designed along the same lines. The walls were of mortar, often faced with small stones which gave the impression of a network (*opus reticulatum*). At the corners and doorways the walls were reinforced with tufa blocks. There might be a second story running around the atrium.

The atrium house looked in upon itself. Its windows giving on the outside world were insignificant. Light and air came in through the open space in the atrium and the peristyle. Complete privacy was assured, and the physical isolation emphasized the unity of the household. The strong ties which bound together members of a Roman family under the supreme authority of the *pater familias* in early republican times seem to have had their natural environment in the Roman house. It was the closed territory of a tight, self-sufficient social unit.

In Pompeii we have many examples of private houses in which the space along the street on each side of the main entrance was used for shops. They were completely separated from the dwelling quarters. There were thousands of these shops in Augustan Rome, of which the great majority were not parts of private houses. They were in their simplest form a row of separate rooms all facing on the street. Each room served as an individual shop and also, in some instances, as the dwelling of the artisan or shopkeeper and his family. Sometimes there were two rows, standing back to back with a common wall or divided by a narrow passageway. The shop might have a mezzanine floor with its own window over the door, serving as a storeroom or as living quarters. It was reached by a ladder within the unit. Others had regular second-story rooms over the shops which were entered from the rooms below or from corridors or balconies. Isolated staircases led to the latter from the street. A portico might stand before a row of shops and its roof serve as the balcony of the second story. When the first basilicas were built in the Roman Forum, they were placed directly behind rows of shops so that the front wall of the basilica became the back wall of the shops. This arrangement can be seen most clearly today in the remains of the Basilica Aemilia.

Obviously, only a small fraction of the population could afford to own private houses. Nor were all the less wealthy forced to live in the places where they exercised their trades or crafts. The problem of shelter for most inhabitants of the city was solved by the erection of apartment houses of several stories built of lime and rubble walls, strengthened by wooden beams. Vitruvius, an architect of the Augustan Age, states plainly that the city had to grow vertically since there was not enough space on the ground to build the innumerable habitations which the city needed. Many of the tenements were poorly built and frequently collapsed. Augustus was providing for public safety when he forbade any building on a public street to be more than seventy-five feet high.

The tenement (*insula*) had grown out of rows of shops which lined the outer sides of a central courtyard. It was a logical step to use the space above the shops for rooms or apartments and to add to these dwelling units some of the area of the central courtyard by building up along its edges. On the street level a typical *insula* presented a façade of shops broken by a passageway leading into the center of the building and a staircase leading directly to the second floor. On this floor a balcony ran around the building from which the rooms could be entered. The approach to rooms on the higher floors was made from corridors which surrounded the light well in the middle.

An *insula* of this sort with one- or two-room apartments sheltered the poorer inhabitants. There were more lavish quarters in the better apartment houses for those who could afford them. Some apartments occupied the entire floor of a building. In the large rookeries there were no open fireplaces; cooking facilities and heating in cold weather were furnished by braziers. There was usually a single pit-latrine under the staircase on the ground floor for the use of all the tenants. Water was not piped in, but it was readily available in the fountains, standing in the city squares and on the street corners, which flowed continuously with water from the aqueducts.

The city's excellent water system was not created in the Augustan Age. When Marcus Agrippa, as aedile, built the Aqua Julia in 33 B.C., four aqueducts were already pouring water into Rome, of which the oldest, the Aqua Appia, had been built in 312 B.C. Under the Republic, the responsibility for the water supply had belonged to the censors, assisted by the aediles. The actual maintenance of the aqueducts was let out to private contractors. Augustus put the entire water system under his close friend and lieutenant Marcus

Agrippa, who became Rome's first permanent water commissioner. Agrippa organized and trained a company of 240 slaves to perform the routine work. In addition to the Julia, he constructed the Aqua Virgo in 19 B.C., which supplied his baths behind the Pantheon. This aqueduct was restored in the Renaissance, and the coins thrown by visitors into the Trevi Fountain are covered by its waters for a short while.

At Agrippa's death in 12 B.C., his band of slaves was inherited by Augustus. He turned them over to the state and reorganized the administration of the water system. Under powers granted him by the Senate, the Emperor appointed a water board consisting of a chairman, the *curator aquarum,* and two assistants, the *adiutores.* Marcus Valerius Corvinus, whom we have mentioned in connection with the urban prefecture, not only accepted the chairmanship, but held it until A.D. 13. Evidently he found nothing in it to wound his republican sensibilities. Both of his assistants were senators, one being of praetorian rank. Their privileges —they were given the right to wear a magistrate's insignia— and duties were spelled out in resolutions of the Senate. But Augustus determined which citizens would be allowed to have water on the basis of the records of Agrippa.

The first purpose of the Roman water system was to supply the general population of the city with an unceasing flow of water in the public fountains. This was not only a matter of supplying a basic necessity on an adequate scale; it was also a matter of sanitation and public health. Only an abundance of water going beyond the normal needs of drinking, cooking, and washing could make it possible to flush away the city's refuse through the sewers. It is no coincidence that Agrippa cleaned the sewers in the year in which he built the Julian aqueduct and then sailed down them to the Tiber. Water supply and refuse disposal were closely connected. Moreover, the public latrines needed an uninterrupted flow of water. The day had not yet arrived of the marble consistorial chambers which embellished even provincial towns in the later Empire. But the principle of immediate removal of waste matter was already firmly established.

The water which was left over after the common needs had been met was sold to individuals who had it piped into their homes from the reservoirs and mains. We can assume that most of the atrium houses were equipped with running water. The more elaborate contained hot rooms and small pools for bathing. The tenement dwellers had to frequent the public baths of Agrippa or the numerous privately operated bathing establishments, which could be entered for a fee.

A walk in the older parts of Naples, even today, will give us a fair idea of the appearance of the older parts of Augustan Rome, the *urbs vetus*. There are the high tenements with little shops or workshops occupying the ground floor. Most of them have only one room opening on the street, but another room may be behind it which serves as the family's living quarters. A door between the shops leads into the central courtyard of the building. Another gives direct access to the stairs by which the upper floors are reached. There may be an arcade over the sidewalk in front of the house, part of which is appropriated by the shopkeepers as a place to display their wares. The roof of the arcade provides a balcony for the second story. The women come down from their rooms or apartments to draw water at a public fountain. Toilets are primitive. Before the installation of gas and electricity, cooking was done on charcoal braziers or rude stoves, and light came from oil lamps.

127

# ROME

The streets are littered with rubbish which is washed down the main sewers from time to time. They are noisy. The smiths and metalworkers hammer out their wares. The street vendors shout and beckon to their stands. There is bargaining and argument at a high pitch. The Vespa and the small car did not add their explosions to the noises of Augustan Rome, but the schoolboys did chant the alphabet in unison and thus contributed their infantile bit to the general din.

Occasionally an impressive doorway stands between the shops. If one of the double doors is open, a glimpse can be caught of a spacious courtyard and the façade of a seventeenth- or eighteenth-century palace, elegant and aloof in the midst of the surrounding squalor. So in Augustan Rome, the passer-by must have peered through the open doors of the vestibule of a great private house into a cool and lofty atrium and beyond it through the *tablinum* to the greenery, fountains, and harmonious columns of a majestic peristyle. Moving on down the street, he might have made a turn into a spacious piazza where a temple or public building, radiant in its marble revetments, symbolized the authority and order, the wealth and splendor of the gods and the state.

As in later times, artisans who made and sold the same articles were inclined to conduct their business in the same part of the city or on the same street. For the small shop was not only the basic unit of distribution, but also that of production. We know, for example, of the streets of the carpenters, the glass blowers, and the perfumers. This feeling of solidarity was also expressed in the formation of trade associations. In a society in which manual labor was considered demeaning, the members of a craft felt a particularly strong urge to come together in a group which would provide some measure of mutual esteem and self-protection.

128

Plan of Imperial Rome, by Lugli and Gismondi (1949)

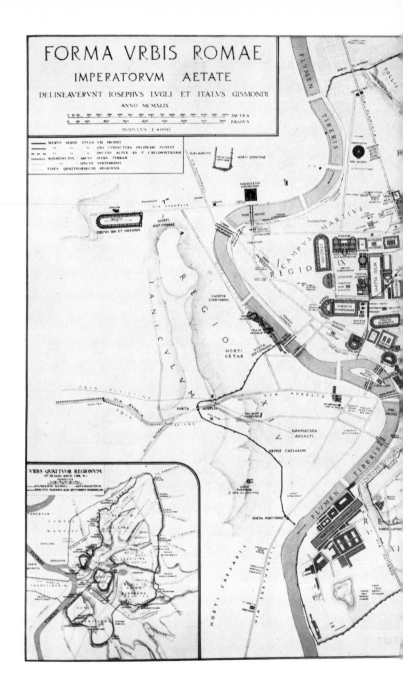

# FORMA VRBIS ROMAE

## IMPERATORVM AETATE

### DELINEAVERVNT IOSEPHVS LVGLI ET ITALVS GISMONDI

ANNO MCMXLIX

METRA
PASSVS

MODVLVS 1:4000

MVRVS SERVII TVLLII VBI PRODIIT
" " " QVI CONIECTVRA DELINEARI POTEST
" " " DVCTVS ALTER AD P. CAELIMONTANAM
AQVAEDVCTVS · ARCVS SVPRA TERRAE
" · SPECVS SVBTERRANEI
FINES QVATTVORDECIM REGIONVM

VRBS QVATTVOR REGIONVM
(IV [?] ANTE CHR. N.)

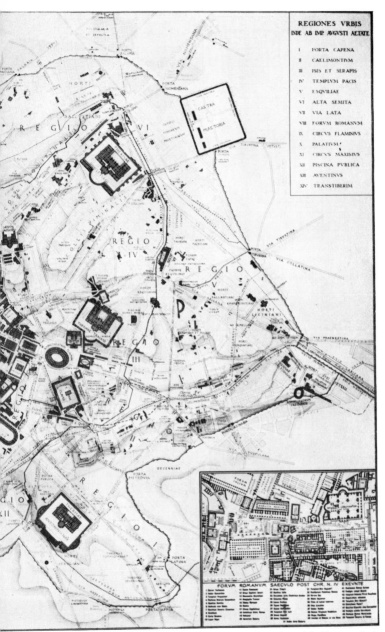

The Romans themselves placed the formation of their earliest trade associations in the reign of Numa Pompilius, the second king of Rome. This simply means that these institutions appeared at an early date in the life of the city.

There is no indication that the Roman trade associations performed economic functions. There was no attempt to bind the individual members to sell at fixed prices or to offer their services at the same wages. Nor do we find in them certain features of the medieval guilds, such as obligatory apprenticeship and standards of capability. Protection of the members' interests was placed in the hands of some influential man who served as a patron. On a less mundane level, a god or goddess was chosen to be the tutelary deity. To this divinity, sacrifices were made by the association as a whole. But this did not prevent the ordinary member from following his own religious inclinations at other times.

The religious sacrifices with which the meetings of an association began were the respectable excuse for the conviviality which followed. The humble laborers and artisans of Rome gathered in their associations to eat and drink, enjoy the friendship and sociability of their equals, and forget for a moment the long hours of hard work which kept them alive. They had no summer or winter dining rooms in which to entertain themselves and their friends. To be sure, there were plenty of bars in which they could pick up a glass of cheap wine and munch a piece of bread and some olives. There were also greasy cookshops in which hot food was available to be eaten on the spot or taken out. But the association dinner, with its modest pretensions to elegance and its atmosphere of friendly decorum, was usually the poor man's only opportunity to emulate the social life of his betters. The associations had officers, and a member who had

129

been elected to fill one of the higher posts could rejoice in the warmth which comes from the favor and confidence of one's fellows.

The associations were not mutual aid societies. They did not take care of their sick, disabled, or unemployed members from the association's treasury, to which all members contributed regularly. But most of them did one thing for a man when he was dead: they gave him a decent burial. The poor man in ancient Rome was not only haunted by the fear of disasters which would reduce his future life on earth to utter misery; he was also forced to worry about his future existence beyond the grave. In order not to float forever in a timeless limbo, he had to be properly cremated or interred. And it would be to his advantage if he was properly remembered at the various festivals such as the *parentalia* or the *rosalia* which were held in honor of the dead.

If a member's association was a very poor one, it might pay for only a part of his funeral. More thriving groups shouldered all expenses and furnished a final resting place in the association's vault. The annual festivals for the dead were celebrated by the associations with appropriate religious ceremonies and commemorative banquets.

The trade association was therefore the worker's club and burial society. For entertainment, exercise, bathing, and relaxation he had at his disposal in the Augustan age the games, the baths of Agrippa, public parks, and the great porticoes and basilicas. But his most pleasant moments must have been those which he spent at the banquets and meetings of his trade association with his fellow craftsmen. This must have been particularly true of the slaves who were allowed to join the associations with their master's permission. There they mingled with freemen and freedmen who were doing the same kind of work on a level of equality. In large households, such as those of members of the imperial family, those assigned to the same tasks were allowed to form their own associations.

There is no evidence that the state exercised any special control over the trade associations until the end of the Republic. Then, when public order broke down and the contests between leaders for power were often translated into class struggles between the "haves" and the "have nots," it was natural for the trade associations to take part in the turbulent politics of the time. Moreover, gangs of ruffians were created to further the ambitions of certain leaders by violent means under the respectable name of trade associations. By 64 B.C. the situation was so alarming that the Senate felt itself compelled to dissolve all associations which acted contrary to the best interests of the state. But Publius Clodius in the year of his tribunate (58 B.C.) brought the political clubs back into existence. The Senate in later decrees and laws attempted to regulate them. It took the firm hand of Julius Caesar to put an end to the prevailing abuses. He suppressed all the associations except those which had a long and legitimate history.

In the period of the civil wars after Caesar's death, new associations sprang up. Augustus took the matter in hand, following the precedent established by Caesar. He dissolved the new associations and allowed the old and legitimate ones to continue. But he also went further. He had a law passed that no new association could be formed without the express permission of the Senate embodied in a formal resolution. This rather mild measure of state control was the beginning of a movement which culminated in the late Empire with the complete subjugation of the workman and his association to the will of the emperor.

Bread, wine, and olive oil were the basic elements of the

Roman diet. In the Augustan Age the grain which fed the city masses was almost exclusively imported from North Africa and Egypt. The deep-sea freighters which could not navigate the Tiber anchored off Ostia, the port of Rome, and their cargoes of grain were transferred to barges which were hauled up the river to the docks and warehouses at the foot of the Aventine. Wine, on the other hand, was largely furnished by Italy. The majority of the city's population undoubtedly drank the ancient equivalent of Frascati, a generic name for the wines produced in the vineyards on the slopes of the Alban Hills. It could be carted into Rome conveniently at small expense. Those who could afford something better turned to wines produced in Campania, of which Falernian was the most famous. There was a brisk coastal trade in Campanian wines, and Falernian of sorts was probably as easily acquired in ancient Rome as Chianti of sorts is in the modern city. Greek wines were a luxury, and there is no indication that they were imported in large quantities. Spanish wines were just beginning to come into the city. At this time, Italy was exporting wine to Gaul.

Olive oil took the place of butter in the Roman diet as the basic fat. It was also used in large quantities for lighting and in connection with exercise and bathing. The city obtained its finest oil from Campania, especially from the land around Venafrum. It was shipped up the coast to Rome with Campania wines. But by the Augustan Age, Spain and Africa were beginning to cut into the Italian market with bulk shipments of oil which was generally considered to be inferior to the Italian. Some olives for eating were imported from overseas, but those most highly prized were sent in from the district of Picenum on the Adriatic.

These articles—oil, wine, and bread—were the staples of the diet of the common people. The oil was distributed in small shops by retailers who bought their supplies from the large importers who had their warehouses near the docks. The owners of the wineshops and bars who dealt in Campanian and overseas wines could turn to the importers of the wine market (the *forum vinarium*), who conducted their business near the modern Monte Testaccio, a sizable hill which was built up in antiquity from broken earthenware containers, such as amphorae, in which oil, wine, and grain were shipped. Many a retailer of local wine must have contracted with a farmer in the neighborhood of the city for his supply. In Augustan times, the farmer's wine cart creaked into Rome from the Alban Hills over the Via Latina, which Valerius Messala had had repaved.

In ancient Rome, baking was a flourishing industry. The baker was also the miller and the distributor. The ordinary man who lived in his shop or in a cramped apartment had no facilities for grinding grain into flour or baking the flour into bread. He had to depend on the baker. So did the citizen on the dole, for he received his allotment in the form of grain. This led to the establishment of rather large bakeries, some of which had state contracts to supply bread to the people whom the state fed directly, such as the public slaves. But the rule was probably the small baker who supplied the needs of his neighborhood daily. He is still the rule in Italy and France where bread is the staff of life and must be both fresh and good. In the atrium houses of the well to do, bread was baked at home, and a large household would have a professionel baker on the household staff.

The poor man did not have to worry about his supply of meat. He rarely saw it on his table except on a holiday. The vegetables and fruit with which he gave variety to his diet came mostly from the truck gardens in the vicinity of the city. But they were also sent up to Rome from Cam-

133

pania and down the Tiber by boat from the interior of Italy. At the vegetable market near the Tiber there was an abundant supply of produce in season on the stands of the individual vendors. The shopper could also frequent the old public market off the Forum or the new one on the Esquiline, built by Augustus and named after his wife Livia.

Most of the meat of Rome was probably driven into the city on the hoof to the ox market (the *forum boarium*). We do not know what facilities the market had for slaughtering and dressing. The retail butchers may have bought their meat there in sides for further splitting in their own shops and stands or bought the animal outright, attending to the processing themselves.

The art of fattening fowl for market and table was well known to the Romans. The great country estates provided game for their owners. Fish was a luxury in the Mediterranean world in classical times as it is today. The rich Romans had their own fish ponds attached to their country villas. Cicero speaks with scorn of certain members of the nobility who, as *piscinarii* (fish-pond owners), put their private comfort before the interests of the state.

Honey furnished the Roman's need for sugar. The finest Italian honey came to the city from Tarentum, the most inferior grade from Sardinia and Corsica. Even the best Italian honey was surpassed by that imported from the slopes of Mount Hybla in Sicily and of Hymettus and Pentelicus in Attica. To provide tartness, fish sauces were in great demand. They were imported in large quantities from Spain and Italian towns south of Rome.

It can be said that with the exception of wheat the food eaten regularly by the ordinary inhabitant of the city was produced in the vicinity of Rome, or at least in Italy, in the Augustan Age. For the wealthy, Roman markets furnished the best of the Mediterranean world, from the oysters of Britain to the plums of Damascus. The provinces naturally shipped their delicacies to the metropolis, where they were in demand among customers who could afford and were willing to pay the best price for them. A society had grown up which was aware of the refinements of the palate, and the art of gastronomy was a serious subject of conversation. Horace might well ridicule the silly pretentiousness, the extravagance, and the ill effects, physical and moral, of the gourmandizing of his day. He might preach the belief that the best sauce is a robust appetite created by healthy exercise and might speak of his own modest meals as banquets of the gods, but his contemporaries who could afford it had quite a different idea of what a divine banquet should offer in the way of delicacies.

Augustus, we are assured, always wore at home a garment made by the women of his family. This was in accordance with the old republican tradition that spinning and weaving were done at home under the direct supervision of the mistress of the house. If Augustus' sister, wife, daughter, and granddaughter humored his whim in this matter, we can be sure that their personal participation in making clothes at home stopped right there. In their own households, as in those of other wealthy people, there were women under competent supervisors who produced the cloth needed by the household. There were also fullers to finish the homespun, dyers to give it color, dressmakers to turn the finished cloth into garments, and maids to keep the wardrobes of their mistresses in order. The luxury fabrics which were imported from the East were bought from special dealers and were cut and sewed by skilled dressmakers.

The poor man's wife did not have the time or the facilities to spin or weave. She and her family frequented a small retailer who kept a stock of rough clothing on hand. This retailer did not weave his own cloth. It was likely woven in the places where the wool was produced in quantity, such as Gaul, the Po valley, Apulia, and the country around Tarentum. There were also establishments which manufactured cheap cloaks and tunics, as well as certain more expensive garments, for which a place could gain a special reputation. The owner of a clothes shop which catered to the poorer classes acquired his stock from the warehouses of the large importers. The dealers of more expensive clothes, who had their shops on the Vicus Tuscus, may have imported both garments and fabrics directly from the manufacturers in the East.

The fullers, laundrymen, cleaners, and dyers of ancient Rome played a large part in the commercial life of the ancient city. The fullers not only cleaned soiled clothing, but also finished homespun. They needed abundant water and special facilities. Only the largest households had this work done at home. The fullers worked in large shops and enjoyed special concessions for drawing water from the public water system. The dyers performed a number of functions. They sold dyes which were imported from the East, gave fresh color to old clothes, and dyed new material to the customer's taste. Some of them probably sold fabrics which they dyed in their own shops.

The *centonarii,* who were both ragpickers and manufacturers of patchwork clothing and blankets, did a flourishing business. Shoemaking was in the hands of individual cobblers who sold their shoes in the workshops where they were made. The craft was highly specialized. There were those who made only heavy boots, or sandals, or ladies' slippers. They acquired their leather from tanneries which processed local and imported skins. Here it was practical to conduct work on a fairly large scale.

The plates and cups of the poor man's table were manufactured in Rome. If he could afford something better, he could buy the figured pottery of a reddish hue which was shipped down to the city from Arretium. The only piece of silver on his table, if he wasn't entirely indigent, was likely to be an ancestral saltcellar, a minor mark of respectability. His simple furniture was made by a local carpenter in his workship. In the Augustan Age, glass was imported.

An army of craftsmen supplied the rich with every luxury. The greatest households would have their own goldsmiths and jewelers. But most of the well to do patronized the craftsmen who designed, made, and sold their own articles. Many of them undoubtedly made jewelry to order. The customer might furnish the raw material. In the time of Augustus, goldsmiths were so numerous that they were divided into two associations—plain goldsmiths and workers in gold leaf. Gold from the mines of Spain was abundant and so was silver. The finest silver plate came from Campania, but large quantities were produced in Rome. The manufacture of silver articles could be conducted successfully by a group, and within some shops the work may have been divided between the casters, engravers, and polishers. But again, we must think of the majority of silversmiths as individuals who manufactured and sold their wares in their own small shops. There was a brisk trade in precious stones and pearls, which were imported from the East by individual jewelers.

The furniture of the wealthy was made by skilled cabinetmakers and was often inlaid with ivory sent to Rome from Africa. Citrus wood was highly prized, especially for tables.

137

It was imported from North Africa. The finest glassware came from the factories of Alexandria and Phoenicia. Arabia furnished incense and India spikenard and malabathrum. Capua was famous for the manufacture of perfumes, which were distributed by retailers in Rome. The association of perfumers was already a hundred years old in the Augustan Age.

In the last century of the Republic, the wealthy began to adorn their households with marble. In the age of Augustus, the quarries of Carrara, in Italy, supplied the demand. The slabs or columns were shipped by sea from Luna to Ostia, where they were put on barges and hauled up the Tiber to the docks of Rome. The contractor who was engaged in making over or erecting a private building could buy his supply from the warehouse of a marble merchant. If his client insisted on something more colorful and expensive, he could find an importer or shipper who would deliver the greenish-tinted blocks from the quarries of Carystus in Euboea (cipolin), or the purplish ones from Synnada in Phrygia (pavonazzo). But the use of marble by private individuals was small compared to that of the Emperor, who boasted that he had found Rome a city of sun-dried brick and had left it one of marble.

The statement is an imperial exaggeration, so far as the city as a whole is concerned. But Augustus did use marble in the public buildings which he built or restored. The temple on the Palatine which he dedicated to Apollo, his tutelary divinity, was built of solid blocks of Carrara marble, and its portico was supported by columns of *giallo antico* (Numidian marble). In other buildings the columns were usually of solid marble, and the walls were covered with marble revetments. Bricks made in the kiln, which strike the visitor to the ruins of ancient Rome and, particularly, ancient Ostia as the standard building material, were just beginning to be used in Augustan Rome. It was not until large parts of the city had to be rebuilt after the great fire of A.D. 64 that fired bricks were used extensively. Apart from the dazzling new and restored public buildings and the interiors of wealthy homes, Augustan Rome must have presented a rather dull appearance of mortar or stone facings, sun-dried bricks, tufa or travertine blocks, and wood.

The sketch we have tried to make of the city's economy during the Augustan Age leads to a few general conclusions. First of all, both production and distribution centered in the small shop or workshop. A few enterprises, such as baking and fulling, might employ more than a handful of men in a single place, but the factory, as we know it today, simply did not exist. The craftsmen and shopkeepers, working individually with a few helpers, supplied the city's needs from their own products, or else processed and distributed imported goods.

The only big business conducted by the state was in grain. A large part of the city's supply came in as tribute from the provinces and was the property of the state. Some of it was distributed to the poorer elements of the population through the dole. The rest must have been sold at a fixed price to the grain dealers of the city. This would have tended to keep retail prices at a fairly uniform level for the kinds of grain which the state sold. When the customer knew exactly what the retailers had paid, it is unlikely that any one of them could have charged higher prices than his competitors for the same article and stayed in business for long. In times of scarcity, the state regulated the prices, for it could not afford to have a hungry and discontented population on its hands. But there is no evidence that in the Augustan Age the retail price of grain was fixed except in emergencies.

Moreover, there seems to have been a flourishing independent trade in wheat. Nothing prevented shippers and importers from taking advantage of attractive prices in centers of production and attempting to make a profit in Rome. Those who could afford to buy the finest Campanian wheat naturally expected to pay more for it than for the ordinary North African variety. Supply and demand set the price, and we can hardly imagine that the state was interested in regulating the cost of any luxury. Consequently, in grain we have an article of commerce in which the state took a very real interest because of its role as the largest importer and because of the effect that scarcity or high prices could have on the bulk of the population. In so far as free competition did not affect the people unfavorably, it was content to leave the traffic in private hands. The attitude of Augustus toward state control of commodities is reflected in a statement which he made at a time when the people complained about the scarcity and high price of wine. He said that his son-in-law Agrippa had taken good care of the situation by constructing more aqueducts so that no one should go thirsty.

From the point of view of those who are accustomed today to finding all kinds of products under one roof, the specialization of the Roman shops seems a grave inconvenience. Even the acquisition of simple foods meant a good deal of moving about for the ordinary woman. We cannot imagine a wealthy matron attending to the routine needs of the household by doing any shopping in person. There were slaves and servants to do these chores for her, when the articles were not made at home. Perhaps she visited her jeweler or a shop for imported fabrics, when she did not prefer to have designs or samples brought to her home for inspection. Or the captain of a ship just in from Spain or the Orient may

have come to her house to offer her some exquisite object
that he had picked up on his travels.

Other less well-to-do women did more of their own er-
rands accompanied by a maid. The poor housewife attended
to her shopping herself. But whoever did the daily shopping,
he or she was assured of fresh food: bread which had been
baked on the day it was bought and fruits and vegetables
which had just been carted to town. There were advantages
then as there are now in Italy and France in buying a day's
supply of food daily.

In the previous chapter, we discussed the upper classes
of Roman society in regard to their functions and position
in the body politic as reorganized under Augustus. Let us
glance at them again from the social and economic point of
view. The senatorial order was both the wealthiest class and
the social aristocracy of the era. The day had passed when
staggering fortunes could be amassed by ruthlessly exploit-
ing a province from the security of a governorship, or by
buying the property of proscribed individuals at a ridiculously low price. Proscriptions on a large scale had terminated with the restored Republic, and one of the basic aims of
the Augustan constitution was to give the provincials decent
government.

But there had been great estates accumulated during the
end of the old Republic which had come down to Augustan
times unscathed, and the heirs to them were wealthy men
indeed. It was also possible to acquire riches legitimately in
the Augustan era. Some of Augustus' generals, such as
Agrippa and Statilius Taurus, laid the foundations of their
fortunes with the share of the booty which came legally to
them from successful military campaigns. Land values were
increasing in the city, and many old families may have pos-

sessed lots on what were once the outskirts or in a suburban area over which the city was expanding. Such real estate can increase fantastically in value in a very short period of time. There must have been speculation in it with handsome returns.

Moreover, who owned the rows of shops and the apartment houses? Certainly not the shopkeepers, or the artisans, or the apartment dwellers. The buildings were capital investments and yielded interest in the form of rent. We know that a large part of the fortune of Crassus, the richest man of the late Republic, was invested in city real estate. It is reasonable to believe that not a few of the senators of the Augustan period had comfortable holdings in town. Obviously a senator did not go about collecting rents or dealing otherwise directly with his tenants. His agents did this for him. But whereas a senator might hesitate, even as a silent partner, to invest in commercial ventures, as activities beneath his dignity, land had always been the most respectable form of wealth. Its exploitation under city conditions in the form of buildings and rents could inflict no social taint.

This does not mean that the Roman senator no longer possessed an estate or estates in Italy or the provinces. In many instances, this was probably the greatest source of wealth of a senatorial family. Evidence of how vast country estates could be in the Augustan Age is furnished by the will of the freedman Gaius Caecilius Isidorus, who died in A.D. 8. He left an estate of 4,116 slaves, 3,600 pair of oxen, 257,000 head of other kinds of livestock, and 60,000,000 sesterces ($3,000,000) in cash. He was undoubtedly a greater landowner than all but the very wealthiest senators.

Finally, moneylending at high interest must have been practiced by a large number of senators. Julius Caesar had established twelve per cent as the legal rate. In A.D. 33 there was a great outcry against those who were charging more. The praetor brought the matter before the Senate, which was greatly embarrassed. For, as Tacitus tells us, there was not a single senator who was free of guilt. Allowing for rhetorical exaggeration, we must still see in the historian's statement the indication that moneylending was a regular source of senatorial wealth. Although the statement is connected with an episode which took place nineteen years after the death of Augustus, the situation had certainly not sprung up over night, nor is it unreasonable to presume that it reflects an activity which was carried on in the Augustan Age.

As for the knights, we hear about them in the late Republic mostly in connection with the great companies which farmed the taxes of Asia and other Eastern provinces. The record is one of unmitigated greed and complete indifference to the interests of the provincials. Caesar finally removed the collection of the tithes of Asia from their hands and thus deprived them of their most abundant source of revenue. Under Augustus, direct taxes were collected by imperial procurators, and although the collection of other taxes might be let out to companies, they were under the supervision of the imperial officials.

Another lucrative form of equestrian business had been the lending of money at usurious rates to provincial municipalities which were hard pressed to meet their financial obligations, especially their payments to the Roman government. Wealthy knights, however, were not the only ones to follow this path to riches. Marcus Junius Brutus, that paragon of noble virtues, lent the town of Salamis, in Cyprus, money at 48 per cent interest per year. He had the decency to act through an intermediary, a Cilician banker named Scaptius, and the indecency to ask Cicero, while he was governor of Cilicia, to help Scaptius recover his illegal

143

interest by force. Under Augustus this kind of flagrant scandal disappeared. The equestrians also formed companies to contract for the erection and repair of public buildings and to operate large enterprises, such as mines.

When Augustus reformed the tax system in the provinces, he cut the wealthy knights off from their most profitable field of investment. But the ones who were able to provide the capital funds needed to organize the big tax-farming companies must always have represented only a fraction of the men in Rome and Italy whose property entitled them to be called Roman knights. We know of many knights who were content to live their lives modestly in the Italian towns in which they were born, attending to their land. Their sons might come to Rome to make a career in politics, and not a few managed to enter the Senate. Whether they did so or remained in their own order, the farms which they inherited were probably their most solid source of income. Some must have owned city real estate. Others engaged in moneylending, and we know of some whom Augustus censured for borrowing at low rates and lending at high. We should expect to know of a large number who owned or were perhaps partners in large businesses, such as shipping, importing, warehousing, or wholesaling. The evidence is slim. This does not preclude that knights did not invest quietly in large commercial ventures, leaving the management to others. The fact was that in the Augustan Age a knight could support himself by entering upon an equestrian career in the army and civil service, for which he received reasonable remuneration. The order under Augustus was becoming a class of officers and civil servants who less and less had to depend on any fortune larger than the 400,000 sesterces of capital which was a prerequisite of the equestrian rank.

Senators and knights formed a social and economic group which was far above the great mass of freemen and freedmen, to say nothing of the slaves. The plebeians worked in the shops, belonged to the trade associations, and inhabited the tenements. A few may have been economically comfortable or even rich. But their chances of mixing socially with members of the two upper classes were practically nonexistent. Their descendants might reach knighthood, or even enter the Senate after a few generations, but they themselves, unless they captured the imperial favor or had the genius of a Horace, which transcended class boundaries, would remain socially where they were born. We have already discussed the composition of the plebs, their political position in the restored Republic, and some of their social and economic activities. We must now look at them again in the light of the dole.

Augustus himself declared that he had once been inclined to abolish the free distributions of grain because they caused agriculture to be neglected, but that he had given up the idea because he was certain that if they were suppressed, they would some day be restored for political reasons. The Emperor was well aware of the demagogic character of the grain laws which had been passed before he came to power. He speaks as if he could have abolished the dole by simple fiat. But nothing, with the possible exception of the halting of the public spectacles, could have so injured his popularity with a very large segment of the Roman people. Indeed, it is more than likely that the abolishment of the dole would have been followed by bloody riots. It would also have been unfair to those citizens who were in honest need of it in order to survive.

Even before the tribunate of Gaius Gracchus (123 B.C.), the Republic had imported grain in time of famine and had sold it to the people at reduced prices. Gracchus proposed a bill which provided that grain should be sold by the state to all the citizen inhabitants of Rome at one-half the market price. The treasury would pay the other half. This was a piece of pure demagogy. The law could not help being a serious obstacle to the successful realization of Gracchus' own agrarian program, which was designed to create healthy agricultural conditions in Italy by splitting up the large estates into small farms which would be owned by those who worked them. It would be more difficult than ever to persuade individuals among the city's poor to abandon the city for hard work on the land. Moreover, since the government would attempt to keep the losses of the treasury to a minimum by importing cheap wheat from abroad, the market for the Italian farmer would be greatly reduced and depressed. Yet, in spite of these results which could be readily foreseen, Gracchus had his bill turned into a law. He needed the support of the common people for his other reforms, and his grain law was the crudest and most effective way of securing it.

The next obvious step was taken by the tribune Publius Clodius in 58 B.C. He had a law passed which provided for the free distribution of a fixed amount of grain monthly to every citizen. There must have been lists kept of those entitled to draw their share, for noncitizens and slaves were not qualified. We cannot imagine that a Cicero or a Crassus had himself inscribed. This was probably true of all senators and knights and more substantial members of the lower classes who did not care to put themselves on the same footing as their poorer fellows.

By 46 B.C. the number of recipients had reached 320,000. Julius Caesar had the number reduced to 150,000 by making a block-to-block canvas of the city's population. By 2

B.C., Augustus had managed to fix the number of recipients at about 200,000, for he tells us in the *Res Gestae* that in this year he made a gift of 60 denarii (240 sesterces) per person to "the plebs who receive public grain" (*plebs frumentaria*) and that slightly more than 200,000 men were involved. In the same chapter, he speaks of giving the same amount of money in 5 B.C. to 320,000 of the urban plebs. If the latter figure represents approximately the plebian population of the city in the fourteen regions, some 62 per cent of this element must have been receiving free grain.

It has been held that when Caesar reduced the number of recipients, certain economic qualifications for eligibility were established, and that possibly the *plebs sordida* alone, the lowest part of the plebeian population, perennially unemployed and indigent, were fed at state expense. This is unlikely. Gracchus himself had seen that his law should in principle apply to all citizens, although in fact it was directed at a class or group. The well to do could be counted on not to take advantage of its benefits. There was no reason to make it even more hateful to the rich and powerful by making it a class measure. By Caesar's time it was generally accepted that the two qualifications for receiving the dole were Roman citizenship and residence in Rome. Caesar probably struck from the lists all those who had crept into them illegally. It is also reasonably certain that, with the possible exception of some widows and orphans, those who received the dole were men who had reached their political majority. They had to share their rations with their dependents.

Let us assume that we have correctly estimated that 62 per cent of the plebeian population received the dole. This is a shocking figure indeed, if, thinking in modern terms, we equate the dole with unemployment and more or less complete poverty. It is also very shocking if we see in all recipients men who preferred eking out a miserable existence at the state's expense to doing an honest day's work when work was available. These are both extreme interpretations.

There were doubtless those in ancient Rome, as there are in every modern city, who would do almost anything to avoid work, regardless of the opportunities offered. These congenital good-for-nothings could take advantage of their Roman citizenship and their residence in the city to keep body and soul together with the grain which the government provided. But the gift was of grain and nothing else. The government did not provide free housing, clothing, or any other food. If a man was lucky, he might be a hanger-on of some wealthy house and receive a handout now and then. He would also receive his share on the occasions when the Emperor chose to exercise largesse. These did not take place regularly. Only an existence of the most abject misery can be imagined for the poor citizen who refused to do any work at all.

There must have been those too who were willing to work, but had no skill or trade to offer. We think first of the small farmers who had been driven from their holdings by conditions which they had no way of resisting. Apart from the brutal ejections which took place in the civil wars before Actium, when many farms were taken away from small landowners to satisfy the veterans' demands for bonuses, there is no reason to believe that the great estates did not continue to grow in Italy under the Augustan peace and to swallow up the lands of the small farmers who could not compete with them. Could Caecilius Isidorus, with four thousand slaves and innumerable livestock, have bought up his vast estates without displacing a considerable number of small farmers? Granted that the farmer was paid for his land, was he likely to look for other acres to farm, or would he rather come to Rome, where he might find other employment and stretch out the money which he had received for his farm with the help of the dole?

Some must have come to Rome bringing to the labor market only a skill in farming of which Rome had no need. Perhaps they also brought with them a certain pride which prevented them from engaging in the more menial tasks. After all, they and their ancestors had been citizens and landowners for a long time. The dole was their legal due, and they could accept it in preference to performing certain tasks until something better turned up.

Finally, there must have been a vast majority of simple citizens who had full-time jobs and found in the dole a welcome addition to their modest earnings. The flourishing shops and workshops of Augustan Rome, the import trade, and the imperial building program demanded an impressive amount of skilled and unskilled labor, and our evidence shows that it was largely furnished by freemen and freedmen, not by slaves. The traditional bleak picture of the common citizens of Rome as a group sunk in a morass of corrupting idleness needs a great deal of retouching.

This does not mean that the dole did not have a demoralizing effect. It undoubtedly did, by making it easier for the worthless to be worthless and to infect others with their faults. But one thing we must keep in mind. For centuries the provinces had enriched the upper classes legitimately and illegitimately. Even when Augustus gave them a more honest and equitable administration, the city continued to profit hugely from their contributions. The dole was the share of the common people of Rome in the wealth of the Empire which their ancestors had created. We cannot blame them too much if they felt within their rights in having this relatively small part of it.

It is worth noting how in this matter of the grain supply and its distribution Augustus attempted originally to use the old republican state machinery which he had inherited. Julius Caesar had raised the number of the college of aediles from four to six by adding two *aediles Cereales,* who were specifically charged with the supply, storage, and distribution of the public grain. Funds were furnished from the public treasury (the *aerarium*), which was controlled by the Senate.

Augustus must have foreseen that two minor magistrates could not attend indefinitely in a satisfactory manner to every aspect of the state's grain supply and its distribution. Yet in the first serious dearth of his principate, he preferred to come to the aid of the people's hunger as an individual benefactor. He tells us, in the *Res Gestae,* that in his eleventh consulship (23 B.C.) he made twelve distributions of grain at his own expense, presumably using the existing administrative machinery. This signal generosity must have whetted the appetite of the people both literally and figuratively. The following year was one of pestilence and famine. The people looked to Augustus to alleviate their woes and attempted to compel him to assume the dictatorship and the responsibility for the grain supply (the *cura annonae*). The precedent of Pompey the Great, who had been given an extraordinary commission to procure grain in 57 B.C. was mentioned. The desire of the people to have Augustus become dictator was motivated in part by the suspicion that the government was being restored to the old nobility. The pressure put upon him to undertake the *cura annonae* was caused by the immediate distress and the belief that he alone could prevent such emergencies in the future.

Augustus refused the dictatorship and reluctantly accepted responsibility for the grain supply. It has been debated whether from that time on he remained responsible for the feeding of Rome. This does not seem to have been the case. Nevertheless, Augustus did separate the function of procurement and storage from that of distribution. To supervise the latter, he had the magistrates in office prepare a list of former praetors, from which two were chosen by lot. (The board was increased to four in 18 B.C.) Through their higher authority and wider experience, they could handle with greater competence the problems of distribution. Moreover, they were extraordinary magistrates, who were answerable to the Senate, and not imperial deputies. The money for the state grain supply continued to be allocated from the state treasury. Presumably after the crisis of 22 B.C. had been surmounted, procurement became once again the function of the *aediles Cereales*.

In A.D. 6 the city was again afflicted by famine. The critical situation caused Augustus to review the entire matter of the city's grain. From his private funds he again undertook to alleviate the dearth, but it must have been doubly clear to him by then that if recurring food crises were to be avoided, the imperial power would have to intervene permanently. For the moment, Augustus appointed two former consuls to supervise every aspect of procurement and distribution. Being his appointments, they were responsible to him. Before his death in A.D. 14, the procurement was placed under a prefect of the equestrian order (the *prefectus annonae*) who was under the direct command of the Emperor. Distribution at Rome continued under the supervision of former praetors. This title, *aedilis Cerealis,* is found as late as the third century A.D., but in the last years of Augustus the aediles had lost any connection with the grain supply.

If we turn now from bread to circuses, following the order of Juvenal, we find that after the death of Julius Caesar in 44 B.C. the Roman public looked forward to at least seventy-six days of free entertainment. It was provided during eight periods of public games (*ludi publici*) which were celebrated every year on fixed days of the different months. For example, the Roman Games, also called the Great Games, were held from September 4 through September 19. Six of these games were old, or relatively old, Roman festivals dedicated to a specific god or goddess. The Roman Games honored the Capitoline Jupiter, the chief deity of the Roman people, and were founded, according to Roman tradition, by Tarquinius Priscus, one of the kings of Rome. The youngest of the six was established at the end of the third century B.C. as part of the cult of the Great Mother of the gods which had recently been brought to Rome from Asia Minor. Although certain acts, such as sacrifices and ritual banquets, reminded the Augustan Roman of the original significance of the games which he attended, by and large he felt them to be a form of entertainment in which pleasure and excitement were the dominating features.

Cornelius Sulla and Julius Caesar added two new games to the traditional list. Sulla commemorated his victory over the Samites at the Colline Gate of Rome in 82 B.C. by establishing annual games of seven days duration. They were dedicated to his personal goddess of victory, Victoria Sullana. The eleven days of games founded by Caesar in 46 B.C. originally honored Venus the Mother, whose temple Caesar inaugurated in his new forum in the same year. Under Augustus they were celebrated from July 20 through July 30 and were known as the Games of the Victory of Caesar.

The Romans themselves distinguished three principal kinds of spectacles: games in the circus (*ludi circenses*), games on the stage (*ludi scaenici*), and gladiatorial shows (*munera gladiatoria*). The fights with wild beasts called "hunts" (*venationes*) belonged in this last category. The combats between gladiators had come to Rome from Etruria and first appear as part of the games celebrated at the funeral of a distinguished man by his family or heirs (*ludi funebres*). In 105 B.C., we hear for the first time of a gladiatorial show produced by regular Roman magistrates—the consuls on this occasion—as a public spectacle. But the gladiatorial show was not incorporated into the program of the regular public games until A.D. 47 under the Emperor Claudius. Despite its increasing popularity in the late Republic and the Augustan Age, it remained an extraordinary event which was added to, but not part of, the regular state entertainment.

Of the seventy-six days of public games, fifty-five were devoted to theatrical performances and seventeen to horse and chariot racing. The remaining four were occupied by ritual banquets and trials of the horses. Augustus was not inclined to increase to any considerable degree the number of annual public games. We hear of only two which he established, each of which was limited to a single day and devoted to racing in the circus. To celebrate the recovery from the Parthians, by skilled diplomatic pressure, of the legionary standards which Crassus and his army had lost in 53 B.C. at the battle of Carrhae, Augustus instituted the Games of Mars (*ludi Martiales*) in connection with the dedication in A.D. 19 of a small shrine to Mars on the Capitoline.

The shrine had been built to house the standards temporarily until the great Temple of Mars in the Forum of Augustus was completed. The latter was dedicated on August 1, 2 B.C., the anniversary of the day on which Antonius died and Egypt was placed under Roman rule. Augustus allowed his grandsons, Gaius and Lucius Caesar, whom he had adopted in 17 B.C., to preside over the racing which was part of the occasion. In the remains of a unique painted calendar from Ostia, the port of Rome, in which various festivals of July and August are depicted as being celebrated by young children, that of August 1 has its place with figures representing Gaius, Lucius, and Augustus himself.

The Emperor made handsome compensation to his fellow citizens for his disinclination to establish new regular games which his successors would be obliged to continue. Suetonius tells us that in the frequency, variety, and magnificence of his spectacles Augustus surpassed all his predecessors. He publicly confessed his passionate interest in shows of all sorts and when present in person concentrated his interest on the event in progress. Julius Caesar had been criticized by the crowd for reading and answering petitions and letters in his seat during performances.

In the *Res Gestae,* Augustus has left us a list of his contributions to the entertainment of the people of Rome. It forms the third part of the central section of the work, which is concerned with the benefits conferred on his fellow citizens by the Emperor. In reviewing it we shall attempt to place the short factual notices within a larger historical context.

Augustus tells us that he held games four times in his own name and twenty-three times in the place of other magistrates. These were the regular annual games, most of which under the Republic had been in charge of the aediles, although on occasion higher magistrates might preside. In principle, the expenses were covered by appropriations from the public treasury, but when they did not suffice, it was incumbent upon the aediles to make up the difference from their private means. More than that, since the aedileship was one of the gates to the higher offices, the praetorship and the consulship, in which a man might hope to restore and increase his fortune through the lucrative provincial governorsips, the aediles attempted to outbid each other for popular favor and future votes by the extravagance of the spectacles which they offered. The point was reached where poorer senators who were unwilling to incur vast debts on the chance that they would reach positions in the future which would allow them to repay them refused to stand for the aedileship.

In the Augustan ladder of offices (*cursus honorum*), patricians were compelled to hold the aedileship before they could stand for the higher magistracies. The tribunate was open only to members of the plebeian families. Augustus, obviously, could not allow honest and able patricians to be deterred from standing for the aedileship by the expenses which the office involved. Nor could he look with favor on a situation which permitted bad or incompetent men to achieve general popularity purely by virtue of lavish expenditures which they could or could not afford. Consequently, in A.D. 22, he transferred the regular public games from the aediles to the college of the praetors, then ten in number, and established reasonable appropriations to cover the costs. He forbade any praetor to spend more than any other from his own funds in order to eliminate extravagant competition. Nevertheless, it was necessary about four years later to place a limit on private subsidies. The praetors were then allowed to contribute three times the sum provided by the state. In 22, the praetors were also forbidden to give gladiatorial shows without the express consent of the Senate, and on no account more than two in each year. The number of gladiators appearing in each show was fixed at a maximum of 120.

By these regulations and by generously paying for games which were given in the names of regular magistrates who were unable to shoulder the financial burden, Augustus attempted to remove the regular games from the sphere of political ambition, while leaving them in their traditional close relation to the city magistrates.

The most unusual celebration which the Augustan Roman was privileged to witness was that of the Secular Games in 17 B.C. From the *Res Gestae* we learn that they were put on by Augustus, with Agrippa as his colleague, in behalf of the board of fifteen men who were charged with the supervision of foreign cults and the Sibylline Books. These games were first celebrated in 249 B.C., when the first Punic war was going badly for the Romans. In three nights a sacrifice was made in a place near the Tiber at an underground altar to Dis Pater, the god who ruled the underworld, and his consort Proserpina. The deities were imported from Greek southern Italy, and the ceremony was a rite of expiation. Of the actual games we know only that horse racing took place. It was vowed that the ceremony would be repeated after a *saeculum* had passed, a period of a hundred years. The vow was fulfilled three years after the lapse of the century in 146.

Augustus discerned that the Secular Games could be made to contribute impressively to the climate of thought and feeling with which he wished to surround his regime. The dark era of the civil wars was over, and a new era of prosperity and peace, a veritable golden age, was opening before Rome and the empire. The Parthians had returned the Roman standards, and the rebellious tribes of north-west Spain had finally been subdued by Agrippa. The larger part of Augustus' program of social legislation designed to protect marriage and the home and to increase the birth rate had become effective. On the other hand, there was much in the past for which atonement had to be made, much which needed to be expiated and buried. This could be done through the traditional ceremony. But to it, elements could be added which would make the Roman realize his present blessings and give him visions of an even more propitious future, a theme emphasized in Augustan literature and art.

Augustus himself settled on the year 17 B.C. Ten years earlier the Republic had been restored, and the new constitution which had been then created had proved its fundamental value. After the great political gesture, it was time to make the gesture of the spirit and the mind. The obstacle to the selection of 17 B.C. was that it could not be made to accord with a system of secular celebrations beginning in 249 B.C. This was surmounted by the creation of a new *saeculum* lasting 110 instead of 100 years which was then made to account for fictitious celebrations on every 110 years since the first in 456 B.C. Even so, the Augustan celebration took place one year too soon, in 17 instead of 16, a discrepancy which has never been satisfactorily explained. Following tradition, the Sibylline Books were duly consulted and under the proper interpretation gave the religious sanction for the festival. The ritual was planned by the distinguished jurist Ateius Capito.

On three successive nights Augustus made sacrifices to the Fates, the Ilithyae (goddesses of childbirth), and Mother Earth, as ordered by the Sibylline Oracle. It is significant that these goddesses were substituted for Dis Pater and Proserpina, the rulers of the kingdom of the dead. The symbolism was that of birth and fertility, for the Fates determined the course of life of the newborn child, the Ilithyae assisted his entrance into the world, and Mother Earth maintained him with her fruits. But the time (night) and the place (the subterranean altar near the Tiber) recalled the old ceremony of expiation. The archaic language of the prayers invoking divine favor on the safety, prosperity, and victory of the Roman people was also anchored in the past. Augustus performed these sacrifices and said these prayers alone. He made it clear that it was his task and his alone to close the old era and to make atonement for it.

The most striking innovations were sacrifices and prayers by day to Jupiter, Juno, and Apollo and Diana, the last two being honored together on the third day. In these rites Augustus was assisted by his son-in-law Agrippa, who was closely associated with him in power. The presence of Agrippa was an indication that Augustus had found the man qualified to help him preserve and increase the blessings of the Roman people and carry on his program of benefactions in the event of his death or disability. The sacrifices to Jupiter and Juno were performed on the first and second days on the Capitoline Hill before the great Temple of Jupiter. Augustus could not fail to give precedence to the head of the Roman pantheon and his consort. But Apollo, the Emperor's tutelary deity, and his sister Diana received a unique tribute before the Temple of Apollo on the Palatine which Augustus had dedicated in 28 B.C. A chorus of twenty-seven boys and twenty-seven young girls sang a hymn specially composed for the occasion by Quintus Horatius Flaccus, who, after the death of Vergil in 19 B.C., was recognized as Rome's greatest poet. The hymn, the *Carmen Saeculare,* has come down to us in Horatian manuscripts. It is both a prayer to the gods of the festival for Rome's future and an encomium of Augustus and his regime. In the Terme Museum at Rome today we can see the remains of an inscription which contains a contemporary account of the Secular Games. Horace is mentioned by name there as the author of the hymn.

Theatrical performances followed all the sacrifices. On the first night, out of deference for tradition, the audience was compelled to stand, for it was only in 55 B.C. that Pompey had built Rome's first permanent theatre of stone with seats for the spectators. A temporary wooden auditorium, probably of bleachers, was erected for their comfort during successive performances. After those of the third day had terminated, a race course was improvised and chariot races were held. This was the formal end of the *ludi* but not of the people's entertainment. After a day of rest (June 4), seven continuous days were devoted to shows, divided among three theatres, horse racing, and animal hunts. These additional games were called "honorary." This should mean that they were paid for by the givers themselves instead of the state treasury, but it is more than likely that here too Augustus met the expenses from his own funds in behalf of the College of Fifteen Men.

In the same chapter of the *Res Gestae,* Augustus tells us of eight gladiatorial shows which he gave, three in his own name and five in the names of his sons and grandsons. He adds that about 10,000 gladiators participated in them. This gives an average of 1,250 to each show. When we recall that the praetors were restricted to a maximum number of 120, we realize the lavishness of the imperial spectacles. There were certainly a few Romans to whom the gladiatorial show was a cruel and inhuman spectacle. But to use the striking phrase of Tacitus, the city Roman appears to have conceived his passion for such entertainment "in his mother's

159

womb." Julius Caesar was a notable enthusiast and increased his popularity with the masses by giving splendid shows. Augustus' own taste ran more to athletic contests, particularly wrestling, and he mitigated the brutality of the gladiatorial combat by forbidding any to be held in which the loser was automatically put to death by his victorious adversary. But whatever repugnance he may have felt toward the more cruel aspects of the gladiatorial shows, he made no decided effort to deprive the people of this form of entertainment. In fact, in celebrating the funeral games of Agrippa in 7 B.C., he not only put on combats between single pairs, but pitted whole groups against each other in a mass bloodletting.

Wild animal fights, in which the animals attacked each other or attacked or were attacked by men and dogs, were introduced into Rome in 186 B.C. They soon grew in popular favor, and the end of the Republic saw a number of elaborate spectacles to which the Roman provinces were made to contribute their most exotic and ferocious beasts. It is worth observing in passing that the Roman public was then accustomed to the sight of certain wild animals which did not appear in Europe again after Roman antiquity until the Renaissance, or even the nineteenth century. Augustus records that he presented the people with twenty-six shows of African animals in which about thirty-five hundred were killed. As the mania for this kind of spectacle increased, whole provinces were virtually emptied of certain wild beasts. It can be set down to profit that more land could be safely cultivated. But there were those who deplored the extermination.

The ugliest aspect of the gladiatorial and animal shows was its effect upon the audience. A combat between professional gladiators or a well-trained animal fighter and a wild beast was certainly a display of skill. But it was inseparably connected with the excitement of bloodshed and death. The ever increasing size of the shows under the Empire is a clear indication that the Roman was measuring his pleasure by the amount of blood spilled before his eyes rather than by the display of professional dexterity. This thirst for the rawest kind of excitement is well illustrated by the practices of throwing the worst criminals to the wild beasts at public shows or of forcing them to fight each other to the death. During a gladiatorial show in the Forum in the Augustan Age, a notorious Sicilian brigand was placed on a platform which was contrived to collapse, precipitating him into a cage of animals that tore him apart. The gruesome theatricality of the event foreshadowed the refinements of cruelty which we meet in the later Empire, when a jaded audience demanded and received ever stronger fare. So far as our information goes, the Augustan shows were quite humane on the whole in comparison with what followed.

It is no wonder, then, that athletic contests in the Greek style seemed rather tame affairs to the Roman public. In spite of his personal interest in them, Augustus offered athletic exhibitions only three times to his fellow citizens. To them he summoned the best athletes from all the world and erected special stands for the audience in the Campus Martius. There were evidently few demands for repeat performances. The Emperor had naturally more success in Greece, where he instituted athletic and musical contests which were held every four years at Actium or, rather, the new city of Nicopolis which he founded on the site to celebrate his victory there. At Rome, the same victory was recalled by a series of games in a four-year cycle which, after their first performance in 28 B.C., were held in turn by the four great colleges of priests—the pontifices, the augurs, the seven men in charge of the sacred banquets, and the fifteen men in charge of the Sibylline Books and foreign cults. Athletic contests were part of these games. They were discontinued after Augustus' death.

Finally, there is one last spectacle which Augustus gave the people and about which he tells us more in the *Res Gestae* than about any of the others. It was a naumachia, or artificial battle at sea. Julius Caesar had set the precedent in 46 B.C. In the Campus Martius he had had a basin excavated capable of floating a large number of warships of two, three, and four banks of oars. These he divided into two fleets representing Tyre and Egypt. He manned them with one thousand marines and two thousand oarsmen and sent them against each other in a naval engagement. The basin was filled up in 43, and no trace of it survives.

Augustus chose the dedication of the Temple of Mars Ultor in 2 B.C. as the occasion for his naumachia. He constructed his basin near the right bank of the Tiber. It was one thousand feet long and eight hundred feet wide, and its water was supplied by a new aqueduct, the Aqua Alsietina, which was expressly built for the purpose. Apart from the rowers, three thousand men participated in the battle of two fleets composed of thirty beaked warships and many more lighter craft. The basin continued in existence until at least A.D. 95, serving for the naval shows of later emperors and as an adornment of a wooded park which Augustus laid out in honor of his grandsons, Gaius and Lucius Caesar.

The places where the various spectacles were held were also the object of Augustus' attention. The most important was the Circus Maximus, remains of which can be seen today at the east end of the valley which lies between the

Palatine and the Aventine Hills. Romans attributed its foundation to the first Tarquin. Augustus mentions it in the *Res Gestae* only in connection with his construction of an imperial box on the side of the Palatine from which he, his family, and his guests could watch the games. The Circus had been enlarged by Julius Caesar to hold 250,000 spectators, and there is no reason to believe that Augustus changed Caesar's general plan when he rebuilt the part of it which had been destroyed by fire in 31.

The Circus was one of Rome's most magnificent buildings in the Augustan Age. Its very size was imposing, about two thousand feet long by three hundred feet wide. The spectators, sitting in three sections of seats which rose behind each other, were separated from the arena by a broad channel of water which protected them from the wild beasts. For although the building was primarily designed for horse and chariot racing, animal and gladiatorial shows were also held there. A wall running lengthwise divided the arena into two parts. On it Augustus placed an obelisk which he had imported from Heliopolis, in Egypt. It stands today in the Piazza del Popolo, where it was transported and re-erected at the end of the sixteenth century. The west side of the building contained the stalls, called "prisons" (*carceres*), in which the contenders were placed before the beginning of a race. At a signal of the presiding magistrate, the doors were thrown open simultaneously and the race began. The building was faced with marble. It was surrounded by a colonnade, at the back of which, under the seats, were shops with living quarters above them. Between them were the entrances and staircases leading to the seats. The vicinity was a haunt for fortunetellers, prostitutes, and other dubious characters in search of customers in the crowd. Horace took pleasure in wandering about in this raffish atmosphere.

Chariot races were also held in the Circus Flaminius at the southern end of the Campus Martius which, according to the latest investigations, was situated close to the Tiber. It could also be used for other kinds of spectacles. In 2 B.C. it was flooded and a crocodile hunt was put on in which thirty-six of the beasts perished. Since it was fairly near the Forum, the people often assembled there to listen to political speeches. Augustus delivered his funeral oration over the body of his stepson Drusus in this circus.

The only stone amphitheater which existed in the Augustan Age was the one built by Statilius Taurus at his own expense. Gladiatorial shows were held not only there, as well as in the circuses, but also in the Saepta. This was the place where the Roman people voted. The Saepta of the Augustan Age had begun to be built by Julius Caesar on a magnificent scale. It was finished and dedicated by Agrippa in 26 B.C. It was surrounded by a portico one mile long and had free space within it for the combats. It is ironical that this monument to the people's political power was erected at the time when that power was rapidly vanishing. At least, the citizens at the gladiatorial shows could support their favorites with a partisanship which could do no harm to the state.

Taurus built his amphitheater at the instigation of Augustus. It reflected the Emperor's policy of persuading his wealthier friends to carry some of the financial burden of the imperial building program. Apart from the satisfaction of achieving popularity during his lifetime for the performance of a public service, the builder could hope that he would be recalled to posterity by the presence of his name on his monument. But there was always the danger that someone in the future would restore the original building and substitute his own name for that of the founder. Augustus could give no guarantees for the future, but he could and did set a precedent for his imperial successors. In the *Res Gestae* he mentions specifically that in reconstructing a colonnade which had been built by a certain Gnaeus Octavius (in 168 B.C.) he allowed the name of the original founder to remain. Nor was this an isolated instance. In the oration which his successor Tiberius delivered at Augustus' funeral he emphasized as an example of the late Emperor's magnanimity that the latter restored all buildings which had fallen into disrepair, but never deprived the original builders of their fame. This policy was scrupulously followed by the Emperor Hadrian about a century later. It is the reason why we read today on the front of the Pantheon the inscription "Marcus Agrippa, the son of Lucius, built [this building] in his third consulship [27 B.C.]." The entire monument was so completely rebuilt by Hadrain about A.D. 126 that it has been virtually impossible up to now to find undisputed remains of Agrippa's work.

At the instigation of the Emperor, Lucius Cornelius Balbus erected a stone theater which was dedicated in 13 B.C. Two years later, Augustus finished another permanent theater, which had been begun by Julius Caesar, in honor of his nephew Marcellus who had died in 23. Although Caesar had planned it in the grandiose manner, Augustus extended its area even further over many lots of property which he bought from private individuals. The principal feature of the inauguration was a performance of the Game of Troy (*lusus Troiae*), an old Roman sacred ceremony which Augustus had revived with a shift of emphasis from its religious to its social and physical aspect. Here again we meet the traditional in a new guise and the blend of myth and actuality, sentiment and practicality, which was a basic characteristic of the Augustan Age.

In the *lusus Troiae,* young sons of aristocratic families were organized into three squadrons of horsemen. Carrying arms, they performed a series of intricate maneuvers, some of which initiated a cavalry engagement. The field was laid out as a labyrinth. The exercise was difficult to execute, and its performance was a rigorous test of a participant's application and dexterity. It also demanded of the individual the ability to function as a member of a highly co-ordinated group. The boys who took part were destined to be the leaders of the Roman people. The training which they underwent gave them a sense of discipline and organized effort as well as physical fitness. But equally important was the obligatory display of their state of achievement before the eyes of the Roman people. The boys were acquiring qualities which they would have to possess later as public leaders. They were being taught at an early age to face the people and have their abilities scrutinized.

The word *Troiae* in the title of the game is connected with a verb of motion and has nothing to do etymologically with the city of Troy. Julius Caesar seems to have been the first to identify the game with the city as part of the Julian propaganda which emphasized the descent of the Romans from the Trojans who came to Latium with Aeneas after the fall of their city to the Greeks and Caesar's own descent from the leader, the son of Venus. In the *Aeneid,* which glorifies the founding of the Roman people in the person of its hero, Vergil retrojects into the mythical past the origin of certain historical institutions of his own day. The Game of Troy was one of them. In Book V, it is the closing ceremony of the games celebrated in Sicily to honor the memory of Aeneas' father Anchises, who had died there a year before. Ascanius-Iulus, the son of Aeneas and the ancestor to whom the Julian family traced back its name, led one of the squadrons and later taught the primitive Latins to play the game, by whom it was passed on to Rome. In the performance at the dedication of the Theater of Marcellus, Gaius Caesar, Augustus' oldest grandson who was then nine years old, took part. We can be sure that he led one of the squadrons, not only as grandson of the Emperor, but as a descendant of the original Iulus.

It would be gratifying to report that the new permanent theaters ushered in a brilliant epoch in the history of Roman drama. This we cannot do unless we are willing to identify brilliance solely with quantity and innovation. The Roman drama reached its peak in the second century B.C. with the tragedies of Ennius, Pacuvius, and Accius and the comedies of Plautus, Caecilius, and Terence. The tragedies were stimulated by Greek plays which furnished the plots and characters. However, they were not slavish translations or even close versions, but new plays, composed by their authors along traditional lines. The same can be said of the comedies which were written in the vein and after the models of the "new" comedy which prevailed in Greece in Hellenistic times. The characters and settings remained Greek; the wit and approach became Italian. A second kind of comedy was invented in which the characters were taken from the life of Italy and the scenes were laid in Italian towns.

In the Augustan Age several first-class writers tried their hands at writing tragedy. We only need mention Varius Rufus, Asinius Pollio, and Ovid. Their dramas were greatly admired by their literary contemporaries, and there can be no doubt that they were written in the classical manner. But how many of them were actually produced on the stage, and not merely read to a group of the literary elite, or passed on to cultivated friends who could be expected to appreciate the finer points? We know that the *Thyestes* of Rufus was

167

performed in 29 B.C. at the games which celebrated Augustus' triumphs. But it is far from certain that the *Medea* of Ovid or the tragedies of Pollio were ever brought before the Roman public.

The conventional tragic material, however, could be used as the scaffolding for spectacular scenes such as battles, processions, triumphs—almost any kind of movement in which the eye would be dazzled by sheer masses of men, animals, costumes, and props. We can assume that the gory episodes which took place off stage in the Greek classical drama were acted out in detail for an audience that was used to the gladitorial show and the animal hunt. Horace complains that even among educated people pleasure had migrated from the ear to the eye.

But in one kind of entertainment it had never left the ear. The Romans loved song—the aria, the solo, the duet—which allowed the actor to display his virtuosity as a singer. Songs were an integral part of Roman tragedy and comedy, but they were separated from each other by passages of prose dialogue. In the Augustan Age a form of presentation began to be adopted which had been developed by the Greeks. The lyric parts of tragedies were torn from their places in the fabric of the dramas to which they belonged, rewritten to give the voice wider opportunities to display its skill, and presented to the public as songs. The singer, however, unlike today's concert artist, came out in the costume of the character whom he portrayed and communicated his emotions and thoughts through action as well as song. Since the two talents of acting and singing were rarely found in one person to the same degree, a division of labor was instituted in which the action was portrayed or danced by a professional dancer while the singer sang the score in the background.

This was the origin of the pantomime which began to

flourish in the Augustan Age under the influence of such famous dancers as the Cilician Pylades and the Alexandrian Bathyllus. The anecdote has come down to us that when Augustus rebuked Pylades for a feud which he was carrying on with Bathyllus, the dancer answered, "It is a good thing for you, Caesar, that the people waste their time on us." Pylades seems to have introduced the full chorus and large orchestras into the pantomime to accompany the dancing. They could entertain with interludes when the dancer was not on the stage. Within a single performance the dancer had to "dance" a number of different roles as the libretto developed. But, more than that, within a single scene he portrayed different characters by instant changes in the expression and style. The characters were usually drawn from the world of myth and legend and were portrayed in the midst of well-known erotic episodes—Ares and Aphrodite caught in adultery by Hephaestus, or the passion of Phaedra for her stepson Hippolytus. It was a form of entertainment in which old material was given a new form which satisfied the crowd's appetite for motion, physical and artistic skill in dance and gesture, melodrama, and erotic themes.

Comedies in the manner of Plautus and his immediate successors continued to be written in the Augustan Age and afterwards. But they were probably composed largely as literary exercises. Gaius Melissus, a freedman of Maecenas, tried to elevate the kind of comedy in which the characters and setting were Italian by transferring the environment of his plays from the common people to the knights. This innovation does not seem to have met with any lasting success. The fact is that neither kind of play could compete in popularity with the Atellane farce and the mime.

The Atellane farce was an old form of theatrical entertainment which had come to Rome from Campania. It was played by stock characters as in the later *commedia dell'arte,* and the lines were originally improvised around some simple plot which had been worked out in advance. In the first half of the first century B.C. we begin to hear of specific writers who made a reputation by writing texts for these farces. But by the middle of the century the farces began to be supplanted by the mimes. Augustus probably took a personal interest in reviving their popularity as part of his program of bringing back old native institutions.

The four principal characters were the old dodderer Pappus, the sly hunchback Dossennus, the oafish glutton Bucco, and the blockhead Maccus. These characters kept their basic traits whatever roles were superimposed on them. Maccus, we know, appeared in one play as an exile, in another as a soldier, in yet a third as a virgin. In each one he was still the same old boob wrestling with and defeated by a new set of circumstances which placed his stupidity in a fresh comic light. There must have been secondary actors, for we have titles like *The Fullers* and *The Vinters* which indicate a larger company. But they probably did little more than furnish new situations for the principals. The dialogue was written in simple verses, and there is very little indication of music or singing. The atmosphere was that of the everyday life of the common people in country and city, given, of course, the twists and exaggerations of low comedy. The coarse and lusty language abounded with juicy phrases and obscene words. Some of the erotic scenes were outrageous and must have been wildly funny.

The mime was by far the most popular form of theatrical entertainment. From the artistic point of view, it belonged with the Atellane farce in the category of low comedy. But it possessed certain elements which gave it a greater general appeal. It was not limited to stock characters, it made use of music, song, and dancing, and last, but far from least, it was the only kind of play in which female parts were played by women. It was a tradition of the mime that the actresses should display their charms generously. The plots were more likely than not to revolve around adultery, and the husband's unexpected return, the agonizing running about of wife and lover, the last minute concealment of the latter, the double talk of the husband and wife must have been as familiar to most Romans as it is to anyone who frequents the burlesque shows today. The stage resounded with the physical assaults which are the basic ingredients of slapstick. For variety, myths were parodied in which gods, goddesses, heroes, and heroines were represented in their all-too-human moments.

The license of the mimes was traditional and accepted. The Vestal Virgins attended, as well as young girls of marriageable age. Augustus, who showed himself the inexorable enemy of adultery in his legislation and who banished his own daughter because of her wanton behavior, came to the performances. The theater audiences, since the time of the Republic, had been quick to pick up a verse which could be aptly applied to one of their political figures and use it as the occasion for a manifestation of their feelings. In one mime of which we hear, the audience went so far as to applaud a verse which it had taken as a highly uncomplimentary allusion to the sexual proclivities of the Emperor. The verse was clearly written with the double meaning in mind and is another striking example of the tolerance which the mime enjoyed.

The number of days within the year which were devoted to public entertainment in the Augustan Age should hardly seem excessive to those who are accustomed to a society in which the vast majority of people do no productive work

171

on two days of every week. It should also be kept in mind that the great masses of entertainment provided by private initiative today on a daily, or almost daily, basis—moving pictures, television, radio, and professional sports—were not available to the inhabitants of ancient Rome. The grim reflections, if any, should come from the quality of the entertainment.

There was little or nothing to balance the strong fare which was designed for pure excitement—the speed and danger of the chariot race, the fighting and bloodshed of the gladiatorial show and animal hunt, and the raw sex of the mimes.

Enormous skill and endless wealth was poured into the performances. The charioteers, gladiators, animal fighters, actors, singers, and dancers were the best the Empire could produce. The parades, scenery, and costumes dazzled the eye. The spectator laughed, applauded, gaped, and admired. He even felt pity and fear—pity for a favorite gladiator who had been defeated, and fear that the suspicious husband would discover the lover hidden in the chest. Surely he must have thought, there will never be a time again of such marvelous shows.

Before ending this chapter on the city, a word must be said about the Augustan building program. A detailed list of the buildings constructed in the Augustan Age with dates of dedication, when known, would serve no good purpose. It will be more profitable to examine a few of the outstanding monuments for their place in the intellectual climate of the period; this we shall do in the next chapter. But here we can appropriately indicate some of the general physical aspects of the program.

In the *Res Gestae,* Augustus mentions some twenty-three buildings which he built or reconstructed, in addition to the eighty-two temples which he restored in his sixth consulate (28 B.C.). To these we must add the monuments erected by members of his immediate family, especially his son-in-law Agrippa, monuments erected at his instigation by non-relatives such as Taurus and Balbus, and monuments erected independently by others to honor themselves or Augustus and members of his family. According to a rough estimate, the buildings of some importance which were newly constructed or restored during the time from the death of Caesar to that of Augustus (44 B.C.–A.D. 14) were about 127 in number.

Julius Caesar had planned to embellish the city in a grandiose manner. He had even dreamed of diverting the Tiber into a new channel beginning at the Mulvian bridge, running along the foot of the Monte Mario, and probably rejoining the old bed where the river makes a bend at Castel San Angelo. This would have added the section of the Prati to the Campus Martius. In Caesar's plan, the Campus would have been built over, whereas the Prati would have become the new exercise field. Part of the plan began to be carried out when Caesar set to work building his magnificent new voting precinct (the Saepta) on the west side of the Via Lata (the modern Via del Corso). It was completed and dedicated by Augustus in 26 B.C. Caesar's assassination prevented the rest of his plan from being carried out.

Augustus did not tamper with the Tiber's natural course. But he followed Caesar in choosing the Campus Martius as the site for new public buildings. The southern part of the Campus, near the old Forum, was already occupied by some large structures such as the Theatre of Pompey and the Circus Flaminius, but the land to the north was largely unencumbered, and most of it lay in the public domain. Unless Augustus was prepared to scatter the new buildings of his era over the residential hills, the Campus was the only convenient land available at the time for a concentration of new buildings. Augustus made plain the direction which his building program would take when he began to build his own mausoleum in the northern part of the Campus Martius between the Via Lata and the Tiber in 28 B.C.

By the time of Julius Caesar, the Roman Forum was unbearably crowded with public buildings, shops, shrines, and statues. Caesar helped relieve the congestion by building another forum to the northwest of the older one. This was the first of the great imperial fora which reached their culmination in the Forum of Trajan. We are told by an ancient source that Caesar did not intend his forum to serve as a market place. Nevertheless, a considerable part of its south side was made up of shops, the remains of which can be seen clearly today. The way in which they are built proves that they were part of the original plan. The tradition of the Italic forum as a market place could not be suddenly discarded.

The Capitoline Hill separated the Roman Forum from the Campus Martius. The Forum of Caesar was the first step in providing a monumental passageway between the two on the north. Curiously enough, Augustus did not complete the task when he built his own forum. This was left for Trajan to accomplish about a hundred years later. Augustus could have added his forum to that of Caesar along the same long axis cutting into the northern slope of the Capitoline and through whatever ridge joined this hill to the Quirinal. Instead, he built his forum at right angles and contiguous to the Forum of Caesar. This location, however, was not chosen without some regard for city planning. The Forum of Augustus offered a monumental and easy approach to the Forum of Caesar, and thence to the Forum Romanum, from some of the most crowded districts of the northern part of the city.

The orientation of the Roman Forum which we see today was the work of Julius Caesar. In 78 B.C., Quintus Lutatius Catulus had given the west end of the Forum a monumental façade by building the Tabularium which served to shelter the public archives. On the south side, Caesar tore down the Basilica Sempronia (built in 170 B.C.) and the "old shops" (*tabernae veteres*) which stood before it and built the magnificent Basilica Julia, which he dedicated in 46 B.C. before it was completely finished. Augustus completed it, but it later burned down and was reconstructed on a larger scale in A.D. 12. This basilica stood between two of the oldest temples of Rome: the Temple of Saturn, the foundation of which was attributed to the period of the kings, or the beginning of the Republic, and the Temple of Castor and Pollux dedicated, according to tradition, in 484. The former was entirely rebuilt by Lucius Munatius Plancus, *de manubiis,* that is, with money realized from the sale of booty which belonged to a conquering general. It was traditional that a general who was awarded a triumph should erect or restore a public building from this source. Plancus celebrated his triumph over the Gauls on December 29, 43 B.C. Tiberius entirely reconstructed the Temple of Castor and rededicated it in his name and that of his dead brother Drusus in A.D. 6. The three white marble columns which are a landmark of the Forum today have survived from the Augustan Age.

On the northern side of the Forum, Caesar began to build a new senate house to take the place of the one destroyed by fire in 52 B.C. Augustus completed the work and dedicated the building in 29. Caesar also built a new rostra, which stood in the middle of the western part of the Forum

and faced the east. The northern side, east of the senate
house, was occupied by the Basilica Aemilia. It was originally built in 79 B.C., but had been splendidly reconstructed
between 55 and 34. Caesar contributed part of his Gallic
booty to the enterprise. It suffered from fire in 14 B.C., and
Augustus and the friends of an Aemilius Paullus, whose
ancestors had built and rebuilt the basilica, shouldered the
expense of the restoration.

Augustus thus found the Roman Forum monumentally
enclosed on three sides. On the west, however, where the
land begins to ascend to the Velia, the ridge between the
Palatine and the Esquiline on which the arch of Titus now
stands, there was nothing comparable to the Tabularium to
arrest the eye and frame the area. The only structure was
a large speaker's platform, the Tribunal Aurelium, over
which the broken line of the back walls of the Regia could
be seen. According to tradition, the Regia had been the palace of the kings of Rome, and by the end of the Republic it
was the official residence of the pontifex maximus, the chief
priest of the state religion.

The assassination of Julius Caesar on March 15, 44, and
the events connected with his funeral and memory gave occasion for the erection of a monument which closed the west
side of the Forum appropriately. It will be recalled that Marcus Antonius brought Caesar's corpse into the Forum and
exhibited it in its mutilated state to the Roman people. His
famous funeral oration so influenced his listeners that they
improvised a funeral pyre and cremated the body on the
spot. The ashes were removed to the family burial ground
in the Campus Martius. At the place of cremation an altar
and a column were erected. The latter was inscribed with
the simple words *parenti patriae* ("to the parent of his country"). The Consul Dolabella soon had these memorials re-

moved. But Caesar's memory was not so easily obliterated.

In 42, when Caesar had already been deified, the triumvirate decided to build a temple to Caesar where he had
been cremated. It seems to have been virtually finished by
34, but the strife and civil war which characterized the end
of this decade delayed its dedication until the year 29. In
the *Res Gestae* Augustus claims that he alone built it.

One of the temple's striking features was a platform about
three and one-half meters high which stood in front of the
temple proper. This took the place of the older Tribunal
Aurelium, which had been pulled down to make way for
the new structure. Behind it the temple stood on an even
higher level.

In its earliest phase, the front of the temple platform,
facing the Forum to the west, was broken at its center by
a semicircular niche in which an altar stood. We can account for this architectural arrangement by assuming that
Octavian wished this altar, dedicated to his deified father,
to stand on the same spot as the altar which Dolabella had
destroyed. In 30 B.C., however, the Senate decreed that the
base of the temple should be adorned with the beaks (rostra) of the ships which had been captured at the battle of
Actium. The niche was then walled up in order to give the
platform or tribunal an unbroken front, and the altar,
partially destroyed and covered from above by the floor of
the tribunal which was extended over the earlier niche, became invisible. Its remains can be seen today in the space
between the two walls which has been cleared by archaeologists.

The central part of the east end of the Forum had now
been given a splendid façade in the Temple of the Deified
Caesar. The space between this temple and that of Castor
to the south was further embellished by a triumphal arch

which the Senate caused to be erected in honor of Augustus after Actium. This arch, with a single passageway, was finished in 29 B.C. The reason for its erection was simply stated in the inscription of the attic: "For the preservation of the state." In 19 it was torn down and a more elaborate arch with three passageways was begun on the same axis, a little to the east, to commemorate Augustus' recovery by diplomatic means of the Roman prisoners and military standards from the Parthians.

The Senate and the people attended to filling the space to the north between the temple and the Basilica Aemilia. The most recent excavations indicate that a monumental arch was erected here in honor of Gaius and Lucius Caesar, the Emperor's grandsons by blood and sons by adoption. It must have been built soon after 2 B.C. It was a prolongation to the south of a sort of open pavillion which has now been identified with the Portico of Gaius and Lucius.

The east side of the Forum was a dynastic monument. It honored the founder, Julius Caesar, his son Augustus, and the two young Caesars whom Augustus intended to make his heirs. The temple reminded the Romans that Augustus was the son of a god and that he traced back his Julian blood to the founder of the Roman people, Aeneas, and his Olympian mother, Venus. The beaks of the ships captured at Actium testified that he had saved the state in war; the south arch signified that he was capable of great deeds in peace. And in the north arch, the people were assured that there were worthy successors to continue the peace and well-being of the Augustan Age.

# V

# RELIGION, MORALS, AND IDEAS

WE HAVE ALREADY SEEN that Augustus awaited the death of Marcus Aemilius Lepidus before allowing himself to be elected pontifex maximus in his place. Augustus had been appointed a simple member of the college of Pontiffs by Julius Caesar in 48 B.C. But during the long period from the election of Lepidus in 44 to his death late in 13, Augustus in theory had been inferior to him in the College. He had been urged on a number of occasions to dismiss Lepidus from his high priesthood and to become in title as well as in fact the head of the state religion. Since priests were elected for life, Augustus' refusal to use his power and popularity to relieve Lepidus of his office has usually been attributed to his respect for an old religious tradition. This was undoubtedly the chief reason for the decision, but it must be added that circumstances made it remarkably easy for him not to break with custom. After his elimination from the triumvirate in 36, Lepidus had been compelled to live in virtual relegation in Circei. Despite his lofty title, he was in no position to interfere with any of Augustus' wishes in sacred matters. The Emperor was universally recognized as the actual religious head of the state, and he acted on the basis of this recognition long before he became pontifex maximus.

In the *Res Gestae,* Augustus refers to the four most important colleges of priests. He was a member of each one of them. Because of the honor which was attached to the higher priesthoods, an effort had been made during the late Republic to distribute them equitably among the members of the noble families. The result was that the same man could not occupy more than one major priesthood. Julius Caesar ignored this arrangement and, besides being pontifex maximus, was an augur and a member of the College of Fifteen Men, which was charged with the custody of the Sibylline Books and the general supervision of foreign cults. Augustus followed the precedent set by his adoptive father. He became an augur between 42 and 40 and a member of the Fifteen Men around 37. Between 16 and 13 he joined the College of Seven Men, who attended to certain sacred banquets and processions. He already belonged to the College of Pontiffs.

Membership in any of these priestly colleges did not interfere with a man's civil life or political career. It was, rather, a distinction which a noble hoped to add to his list of high political offices. Under the Republic, the pontifex maximus was often the leader of the Senate, and from Augustus on, this highest priesthood was held regularly by the emperors. What we have already said about the lives of Caesar, Lepidus, and Augustus has shown how civil and military activities of all kinds were considered completely compatible with the highest priesthood in Rome.

There were priesthoods, however, which imposed serious restrictions on the freedom of action and movement of their priests. These were the venerable priesthoods of Jupiter, Mars, and Quirinus, and that of the *rex sacrorum.* The priest of Jupiter, the flamen Dialis, in particular, was hedged about by archaic taboos. We need not dwell on the fact that his hair could be cut only by a bronze knife or that the posts of his bed had to be surrounded by earth. To an ambitious man the important thing was that the priest of Jupiter could not absent himself from Rome for more than two or three nights. This meant that he could not hold a post in the provinces which could lead to wealth and fame. No wonder, then, that as early as the second century B.C. it was difficult to find suitable candidates for the office. When Augustus finally found a properly qualified man to fill it, it had been vacant for some seventy-five years.

There were also a number of old religious sodalities which had ceased to perform their antiquated rites or performed them with more attention to their purely formal features than to their original spirit and meaning. Augustus dutifully became an Arval brother, a member of the sodality of Titus Tatius, and a fetial priest. His presence breathed new life into these vestigial remains of primitive Roman religion. He was even able to make political use of the rites of one of them. When war was declared against Cleopatra in 32, Augustus entered the Temple of Bellona as a fetial priest and there performed all the preliminary rites connected with a formal declaration of war. Under the early Republic, the fetial priests had been charged with this function and also with the conclusion of peace treaties. These had subsequently become purely political matters which were handled by the Senate and magistrates long before the Augustan Age. By reviving the fetial rites, Augustus not only lent solemnity to the occasion, but also strengthened the idea that this was a just and unavoidable war waged solely against a foreign enemy.

During the late Republic and the period of civil wars, a large number of religious buildings had been allowed to fall into a shameful state of disrepair. In one of his gloomiest

181

odes Horace speaks of the crumbling temples and shrines and the cult statues black with smoke. The ode was certainly written before 28 B.C. when Augustus, according to his own report, repaired eighty-two temples. This was the indispensable first step in a religious revival. It gave tangible and visible proof that the Emperor was seriously concerned with the city's religious life and was willing to spend large amounts from his personal funds to rehabilitate it. In the future the houses of the gods would be properly maintained.

The Roman people, however, were shown that they were expected to participate in this part of the religious program. The Emperor with his vast wealth would carry almost all of the financial burden. But simple citizens could make modest contributions according to their means. They were asked to do so by the Emperor on a yearly basis, and in one of the historians we have a description of him holding out his cupped hand to receive the pennies of the poor. It is worth noting that the Emperor decided how the money was to be spent. He was inclined to buy statues of the gods with it.

We have already glanced at Augustus' personal participation in religious colleges and sodalities. His chief religious problem after the restoration of the temples was to restore the prestige of those bodies, especially the higher priesthoods, by filling them with men who enjoyed respect. During the period of the triumvirate, priesthoods had been handed out rather indiscriminately as political rewards. The unworthy among the recipients could not be dismissed, but new members could be more carefully scrutinized. Moreover, a difficulty was caused by the fact that the patrician families were dying out. Certain priesthoods, such as that of Jupiter, could be held only by patricians, and in the four great priestly colleges it had long been customary to include about an equal number of patricians and plebeians.

This balance had been seriously disturbed between the years 44 and 29, when the plebeians far outnumbered the patricians.

Two pieces of legislation gave Augustus the means to come to terms with these problems. In 29, he was given the power to create patricians and to appoint all priests, even in excess of the traditional number of members of any given college. Augustus made use of the first provision to restore the old balance between patrician and plebeian priests in all colleges. By virtue of the second he increased their size. This allowed him to reward a large number of men with the honor of a priesthood. The body of priests rapidly became again a body composed of members of the senatorial nobility which a new man, that is a man who did not have a consular ancestor, found it increasingly difficult to enter. Augustus tells us in the *Res Gestae* that 700 senators served under his standards at Actium of whom 83 later became consuls and about 170 became priests. Augustus did not forget his friends.

The priesthoods which were surrounded by irksome restrictions were still unpopular. We have seen that Augustus had difficulty in finding a properly qualified patrician who was willing to become the priest of Jupiter. His means of persuasion included some mitigation of the severest taboos and the promise of a suffect consulship in the following year. But the priest was still unable to hold a provincial governorship.

There was also difficulty in finding properly qualified girls to serve the cult of Vesta. The trouble began with the parents rather than with the girls themselves. Both parents of a future Vestal Virgin had to be alive and had to have been married by the old religious rite of *confarreatio*. This rite was practiced almost exclusively by patricians, when it was prac-

183

ticed at all. Divorced parents militated against a girl's eligibility. These restrictions limited considerably the number of fathers who could offer their daughters as candidates to the pontifex maximus.

A Vestal was chosen between the ages of six and ten and on being inaugurated was freed from the legal power of her father. She was obligated to remain a Vestal for thirty years. During the period of her office, she enjoyed many legal privileges and civil honors which set her above all other Roman women. But she was also constrained to a life of the strictest chastity, and for deviating from it, she was cruelly punished by being buried alive. After her thirty obligatory years had passed, she could be relieved, on request, of her religious functions and restrictions and would then be free to marry, or, if she preferred, she could remain a Vestal. By this time she was well beyond the normal marrying age of a Roman girl and had presumably adjusted herself to the advantages and limitations of a Vestal's life. Vestals were inclined to remain in their cult and in the chastity which it continued to impose.

It is understandable that a father who was qualified to offer his daughter as a future Vestal Virgin might have strong feelings of hesitancy about doing so. Senatorial families were not likely to be large at that time, and if a daughter was the only child, her consecration to the cult of Vesta would end the propagation of the family's blood. On pure grounds of affection a father might be loath to deprive his daughter of the normal blessings of married life. A daughter also through a well-arranged marriage could bring to her family advantageous alliances in the fields of finance and politics. We are told that on a certain occasion when it became necessary to choose a new Vestal to take the place of one who had died, the Emperor was besieged by fathers who begged not to have their daughters considered as candidates. The situation is not entirely clear, but we can assume that these men knew that their daughters were thoroughly qualified and were trying to forestall any imperial suggestion that they be offered voluntarily. Augustus countered by swearing that if one of his granddaughters had been of the proper age, he would have offered her himself. This was an impressive gesture, but he had to face the facts and increase the Vestal's prerogatives. Just how we do not know. It was probably in some way that compensated the families for the loss of their daughters.

Augustus restored the Lupercal, the grotto on the flank of the Palatine where Romulus and Remus were said to have been suckled by the wolf, and reinstituted the ancient rite of the Luperci, the Wolf-Averters, by which they purified the site of the original city, the Palatine, by running around it. In the late Republic the sodality had become a club of younger men who were conspicuous for their high spirits and wild behavior. The membership had deteriorated socially, and under Caesar even freedmen were admitted. Augustus restricted the membership to knights.

He also revived the *augurium salutis* in 29 when the doors of the Temple of Janus were closed to signify that peace reigned in the Roman world. The *augurium* could only be taken when a Roman army was not making preparations for war or engaged in combat. In the Augustan Age it was the most solemn prayer which could be made for the safety of the Roman people.

The temple of Jupiter Feretrius was thought to have been built by Romulus to celebrate his victory in hand-to-hand combat over Acro, king of the Caeninenses. The engagement was placed at the head of the long list of Roman triumphs which was composed under Augustus. Romulus

185

placed the spoils which he had taken from Acro in the new temple. This established a precedent, and twice thereafter Roman commanders who had killed enemy kings with their own hands placed the armor stripped from the bodies of their adversaries in the same temple.

The building had long been neglected and was even roofless when it was restored by Augustus around 32 B.C. The tradition connected with it soon posed a problem. Marcus Licinius Crassus, who had been Augustus' colleague in the consulship of 30 B.C., was fortunate enough to kill an enemy king while fighting in Macedonia in the following year. He claimed a triumph and the right to deposit his spoils in the Temple of Jupiter Feretrius. Augustus was not pleased. He himself had just celebrated his three triumphs in 29, and, magnificent as they had been, he had not been able to crown them by dedicating to Jupiter Feretrius any spoils acquired through his personal valor. Crassus was a member of a very distinguished republican family who had come over rather late to the side of Augustus. With his spoils he would walk in his triumph like a new Romulus. To Augustus, if there was to be any new Romulus, it was to be himself. He granted Crassus the honor of a triumph, but by a dubious piece of antiquarian research discovered a technicality which prevented him from dedicating his spoils in the temple.

Augustus restored the Temple of the Penates on the Velia, the ridge connecting the Palatine and the Esquiline at the top of which the Arch of Titus now stands. The cult of the Penates was both private and public. In families, they were originally worshiped as deities who presided over the storeroom of the house and its contents. By natural extension, they were soon considered to be the guardians of the entire house. The family hearth was their altar. The Roman people, as a household, also had their Penates. This is only one example of the many parallels which prevailed in ancient Rome between private and public institutions, both religious and secular. We know for certain that a Temple of the Penates existed in Rome on the Velia as early as the second half of the third century B.C. Its origin probably lay in a far earlier period.

In the time of Augustus, the statues of two young men seated and holding spears could be seen in the Temple. They were portrayed in a way which allowed them to be identified as the twin gods Castor and Pollux, who had their own temple farther down in the Forum. An inscription on the base assured the visitor that these were the Great Penates. Even after the legend had been fully formed that the true Penates, which Aeneas had brought from Troy, were preserved in the Latin city of Lavinium, which Aeneas was believed to have founded, Romans must have considered the gods on the Velia the Penates of the Roman family.

It is worth observing that Augustus did not attempt to tamper with this old conviction. Since Aeneas was not only the ancestor of the Roman people as a whole, but also the ancestor of Augustus in particular, so Aeneas' Penates belonged to both. If Augustus had transferred them from Lavinium to Rome—they seem to have been statuettes of wood or bronze—and placed them in the reconstructed temple on the Velia, he would have established a visible religious connection between himself and all his fellow Romans. But an old custom stood in his way. For centuries, the Roman higher magistrates, on taking office, had traveled to Lavinium to renew a treaty with the city and to sacrifice to Vesta and the Penates. The removal of the latter to Rome would have caused an offensive breach in a tradition which was probably older than the legend which associated the local Penates of Lavinium with the presence of Aeneas there.

Moreover, the Roman people had the right to their own ancient Penates, whom they had worshiped long before Aeneas had been enthroned as the principal ancestor. Augustus not only let matters stand, but showed his respect for the Roman Penates by his reconstruction of their temple.

In all these acts by Augustus we can clearly discern an outstanding purpose: to restore the older religious institutions of the Roman people and to give them a new dignity and vigor. The person of the Emperor was involved whether he paid for the reconstruction of a temple or bestowed his prestige on a priestly college by his presence in it or by improving the general quality of its membership. There is another side, however, to Augustus' activity in the sphere of religion which is not so easily defined. In it, Augustus placed himself in a close and personal relation with specific gods, either through events which were connected with the origin of his family in the legendary past or through personal experiences. Julius Caesar had led the way in using the mythical descent of the Julian family as an instrument of dynastic propaganda. Augustus continued his work with the modifications and expansions which seemed necessary or appropriate. But in the elevation of a cult of a god who had come to his personal assistance, he became more of an innovator and, on occasion, broke with tradition. In this connection the Emperor's relation to the cult of Apollo first attracts our attention.

The cult of Apollo was far from new at Rome. In 431 B.C., a temple was dedicated to him which was situated near the later Theater of Marcellus. It had been rebuilt, probably between 36 and 33, by Gaius Sosius, a strong supporter of Marcus Antonius, with the booty which he had obtained in a war against the Jews. Augustus made much of his augurate in the early years of his triumvirate. It placed him at least on the same priestly footing as Antonius, although he was below Lepidus, the pontifex maximus. Apollo was the god of prophecy in general. In particular, he inspired the Sibyls, his prophets. When Augustus became a member of the College of Fifteen Men, who had charge of the Sibylline Books, he was brought closer to Apollo. Perhaps his entrance into this college explains why he vowed to build a new temple in honor of the god if he was victorious in his war with Sextus Pompeius in 36. It is likely that it was intended to rival the reconstruction of the old temple by the Antonian Sosius.

Be that as it may, it was the outcome of the battle of Actium which established Apollo as Augustus' tutelary deity. A temple of Apollo overlooked the sea where the battle took place, and Augustus gave the god the credit for his victory. Following a Hellenistic custom, he dedicated to him ten of the ships which he had captured. He also instituted a cycle of Actian games. It was then a short step to the poetic fiction of Vergil and Propertius, in which Apollo the Archer personally intervened on the side of Augustus against the hordes of the East and their monstrous gods. People began to forget the circumstances of the original vow and saw in the temple on the Palatine a symbol of Augustus' gratitude to Apollo for the assistance which he had given him in winning the decisive battle of his career.

The Palatine Temple of Apollo was dedicated on October 9, 28 B.C. Unfortunately, students of Roman topography have not been able to agree on its location on the hill. Perhaps the latest excavations behind the house of Livia will furnish evidence to settle the problem. However, its general appearance can be reconstructed from literary documents.

If we had approached the temple as the Augustan poet

Propertius did at the time of its dedication, we should first have seen a gilded portico supported by columns of *giallo antico*. Statues of the fifty daughters of Danaus stood in the intercolumnations facing the equestrian statues of their husbands, the sons of Aegyptus, whom they killed on their wedding night. Statues of historical Romans of outstanding talent were placed on the roof of the portico over the capitals of the columns. At some place under the portico, probably in the center, on the same axis as the entrance to the temple, stood a statue of Apollo with his lyre. A library which was divided into Greek and Latin sections was connected with the portico.

One passed through the portico into an open courtyard. An altar occupied its center surrounded by four oxen, the work of the sculptor Myron. The temple behind the courtyard was built entirely of Carrara marble. The doors were inlaid with ivory carved to represent the legend of Niobe and the defeat of the Gauls at Delphi. The chariot of the sun stood on the peak of the gable. Within the temple, the cult statue of Apollo, by Scopas, was flanked by those of his mother Latona and his sister Diana. At the end of the Eighth Book of the *Aeneid,* Vergil describes a shield made by the god Vulcan for Aeneas. One of the large interior panels portrays Augustus at the entrance of the temple observing the gifts brought to him by the peoples of the world in a long procession and affixing them to the temple's proud doors. The picture is poetic, but behind it lay the fact that Augustus endowed the temple with many gifts. In the *Res Gestae* he tells us that about eighty statues of himself on foot, mounted, and in four-horse chariots stood in the city. He had them removed and melted down, and from the money received for the bullion he had gold gifts made which he deposited in the Palatine Temple of Apollo in his own name and in those of the persons who had originally erected the statues.

About 18 B.C. the new temple received a signal honor. The Sibylline Books, which contained the "fate of Rome," were transferred from the Capitoline Temple of Jupiter to the Palatine Temple of Apollo, where they were deposited in the base of the cult statue of the god. As part of this revolutionary change Augustus had over two thousand prophetic books collected and burned which did not possess the marks of authenticity. He thus aimed a blow at a charlatanism which exploited the superstition of the masses and placed the official prophecies of the state in a well-defined, separate category. He further enhanced their authenticity by having them scrutinized for intrusions of extraneous material. Genuine parts of the text which had become illegible because of age were recopied. The work was done by the College of Fifteen Men, of which Augustus was a member. It was the same board which was charged with the administration of the secular games in 17 B.C.

It would almost appear as if the "fate of Rome" had been taken out of the hands of Jupiter Optimus Maximus and placed in those of the Emperor's personal god. Certainly the religious traditionalist Augustus could not have entertained the idea of dethroning Jupiter from his position of supremacy in the Roman Pantheon. We know of magnificent gifts which Augustus deposited in the god's venerable temple on the Palatine. But he could never make Jupiter his tutelary deity. For centuries the god had watched over all Romans and their state. Moreover, the Jupiter of the Capitoline Hill itself, the fortress of the original city, had always been connected with warfare. The triumphal procession terminated at the temple of Jupiter Capitolinus, and the general celebrating the triumph, dressed in the garb which the god wore in his statue, offered him his crown. The god of battles and Roman might had helped him to his victory.

But the period after Actium was to be a period of peace, specifically, the *pax Augusta*. Apollo had shown himself in his role of warrior at Actium so that a lasting peace should reign after Augustus' victory. The poets had shown that the god was then fighting on the side of enlightenment and order, as when in an earlier age he stood in the ranks of the Olympians against the brute force of the Giants and Titans. He could now return to his pre-eminent role as the civilizer, the protector of the peaceful arts, and the leader of the Muses. For it was the Muses, as Horace knew, who gave peaceful counsel and rejoiced in giving it. They gave encouragement to Augustus when he sought to finish his warlike tasks. The statue of Apollo holding his lyre under the portico of the Palatine temple, the statues of the talented men placed above it, and the works of art which adorned all parts of the building, and the Greek and Latin libraries which were part of the complex spoke of a new era in which the arts could flourish peacefully under the god and his mortal favorite. The Temple of Apollo on the Palatine could not and was not intended to supersede the greatest temple of Rome's greatest god. It was meant to be a new center for religious interest which symbolized present and future blessings. It recalled that an age of force had given way to an age of order and reason. In the Sibylline Books the "fate of Rome" had been placed under peaceful auspices. The Apollo of the Palatine was the Apollo of the secular games which introduced a new era.

On September 1, 22 B.C., Augustus dedicated a new temple to Jupiter Tonans (the Thunderer) on the Capitoline. In the course of a military campaign which he was conducting against the Cantabrians in northwest Spain in 26, his litter was grazed by a bolt of lightning which killed a slave who was standing near him. Augustus vowed the construction of the temple as an act of gratitude for his escape. The temple, like that of the Palatine Apollo, was closely related to the Emperor's person. Suetonius reports that Jupiter Capitolinus appeared to Augustus in a dream and complained that his worshipers were being taken from him, whereupon the Emperor replied that Tonans had been placed by his side as his doorkeeper. This simply indicates that the two temples were in close proximity and the people, as is natural, were crowding in to see the new building. Those who would like to find in Augustus the deliberate intention of detracting from the supremacy of the old Jupiter have interpreted the creation of the new temple on the Capitoline as an act of rivalry. But in this connection it should be recalled that Jupiter was originally the god of the heavens and the weather and that in building the Temple of Tonans on the Capitoline Augustus was reviving the oldest aspect of Jupiter Capitolinus. The temple was proof not only that Augustus revered the great god of the Capitoline but also that he personally stood under his protection.

When Augustus became pontifex maximus in 12 B.C., he refused to dwell in the *domus publica,* the official residence of the pontifex maximus near the Regia and the shrine of Vesta, of whose cult he was the high priest. Augustus made part of his house on the Palatine public property in order to conform to the rule that the pontifex should live in a house owned by the state. For decades it was believed that on April 28, 12 B.C., the Emperor dedicated an altar and a shrine to Vesta in this new *domus publica.* A famous base in the Correale Museum at Sorrento appeared to confirm the belief. It is adorned with reliefs portraying or reflecting certain religious events of the Augustan Age. One of them undoubtedly represents the consecration of a temple of Vesta, and since the others are concerned with cults on the Palatine, it was naturally assumed that we had here a sculptural account of the consecration of the Augustan shrine of the Palatine Vesta. This erection of a new shrine of Vesta was taken as a conspicuous break with tradition and an attempt on the Emperor's part to tamper in his own interests with a public cult. The cult of Vesta was one of the oldest in Roman religion, the goddess was the Vesta of the Roman people, and there had always been but one shrine belonging to her, the one at the southeast edge of the old Forum.

Unfortunately for this elaborate hypothesis, it has recently been shown that it was ultimately based on an incorrect restoration of a lacuna in one of the ancient Roman calendars. Augustus did not build a rival shrine to Vesta, but erected an altar and a statue of the goddess in his *domus publica,* which he had every right to do. Consequently the shrine depicted in the Sorrento relief must represent the reconsecration of the shrine near the old Forum. We know that it was damaged by fire in 14 B.C., and the foundations which we have today can be traced back to the Augustan Age. The false reading of the calendar made Augustus less of a traditionalist than he actually was in religious matters.

In the preceding chapter we had occasion to point out that the inclusion of Augustus' genius in the worship accorded to the Lares was not a form of deification. The Emperor's policy regarding himself in the provinces is well known: he did not permit temples to be dedicated to him unless they were also dedicated to the goddess Roma. In the eastern part of the Empire the inhabitants had for centuries bestowed divine honors on their rulers. They were quite content to honor the Romans who took the place of their native kings in the same way. To Augustus, his deification in the East was probably a matter of indifference from the religious point of view. It was a way of feeling and thinking which could do no harm. But politically, it could do a great deal of good for the Empire. The provinces and municipalities could rally around the worship of the Emperor and the deified capital city. This joint cult would be felt as a unified cult in which the living and divine Emperor was the embodiment of Rome and the Empire. Individual Greek cities are known to have forgotten Rome and worshiped the Emperor alone.

In the Western provinces, where there was no tradition of ruler worship, Rome took the initiative. The most famous example is the dedication of an altar, probably with an adjoining temple, to Rome and Augustus at Lugdunum (modern Lyon, in France) by Drusus, the stepson of the Emperor, in 12 B.C. Delegates from the sixty tribes of the three Gauls gathered there to elect the priest and to pay religious homage to Rome and Augustus. The meetings also had a political flavor in that the delegates exchanged views on provincial affairs and were entitled to reward governors with statues and honorific degrees or to bring complaints of maladministration against them before the Emperor. The institution of provincial councils was primarily a matter of religion and loyalty. But it also gave a province as a whole a representative body which, feeble as it was in actual power, served as a voice which the Emperor could not afford to ignore.

In Rome and Italy there was no native tradition of a divine ruler. The educated Roman was familiar with the belief that the great man, the hero, might become a god after his death as a reward for his benefactions upon earth. In a burst of enthusiasm Horace could identify the living Augustus with Mercury and Vergil and proclaim him a true god. This was the poetic imagination at work. The poets were to be listened to more seriously when they spoke of Augustus' place among the gods after his death. In fact, some coins struck early in Augustus' regime have a symbol indicating his eventual apotheosis. Julius Caesar had been approaching the position of a Hellenistic monarch, including divine honors, at the time of his death. He was assassinated by men who would not tolerate an absolute monarch at Rome. But there was little or no opposition to his deification after his death, and Augustus proudly called himself *Divi filius,* "the Son of the Deified." As it had been imperative for Augustus to keep his new constitution free of any taint of monarchy or tyranny, so had his position in the religious thinking of his countrymen to be officially divorced from pretensions to divinity while he was alive.

Augustus was generally successful in avoiding outright divine honors in Rome. It was not an easy task, since parts of the population were eager, or at least willing, to press such honors upon him. The elements of Oriental extraction would have found it no more than natural to worship him as a divinity on earth, the subservient could hope to flatter him with honors belonging to a god, and there were many who saw behind his benefactions to the Roman world a divine power working through its elected human being. To them, an aura of divinity surrounded and informed the mortal man, and at times the lines between the source and its instrument were likely to be blurred.

Even Agrippa wished to name the Pantheon after Augustus and to place his statue among those of the gods under the great rotunda. Augustus refused to accept this implication of divinity, and the statue of the deified Julius was placed in the shrine itself, probably close to those of Mars and Venus, whereas statues of Augustus and Agrippa were placed in the vestibule. Yearly sacrifices were performed by order of the Senate at altars set up to honor the Emperor's return from Syria in 19 B.C. and from the Western provinces in 13. But the sacrifices were made to the goddess who presided over the altars—Fortuna Redux and Pax Augusta. Concerning the latter, we must note the close connection with the Emperor. The goddess Peace was not merely a deified abstraction, a quality which had been given a divine existence of its own which operated among, on, and through mortal beings, but rather was the deification of a certain kind of peace, the kind created by Augustus and identified with him. A concrete state of affairs, a deified abstraction, and the Emperor had been blended into one.

We are likely to think of a religious revival as a spiritual revival which moves men in their hearts and minds. In the Christian conviction it is largely a renovation of faith, a strengthening of right thinking, and a purification of the inner self from the dross of the world. We can hardly speak of the Augustan religious revival in these Christian terms. Traditional Roman religion was a highly formalized complex of rites designed to keep the gods and the state and the gods and the individual in a proper relationship.

The Roman's attitude toward his gods has been summarized in the formula *do ut des*—"I give [to you the god] so that you may give [to me the mortal]." This emphasizes the legalistic and contractual aspect of Roman religion, which was indeed a powerful element in it. But like all such pithy characterizations, it does not do justice to the whole. When we look at the individuals of the Augustan Age, we find simple faith, extreme scepticism, rationalization, habit, and superstition determining the basic outlook of different individuals and also combined in varying degrees in the same person.

From the beginning of the second century B.C., Rome had been exposed to the culture of Greece. In the religious sphere this led to a fusion of the principal divinities of Greece and Rome. Juno and Hera, Venus and Aphrodite, Mercury and Hermes became the same divinities. In the process, however, the Roman gods became Hellenized. The Greek myths, attributes, and spheres of direct influence were attached to them, and they were portrayed in the plastic arts as the types established by generations of Greek artists. In the intellectual field, Greek rationalism exercised a profound influence on the governing class. Its members felt that they had been emancipated from the naïve beliefs and practices of their ancestors and were now free to adopt or devise a new attitude toward religious affairs. Yet, it was generally felt that this was a privilege that should be reserved for the enlightened and that the traditional religion was a good thing for the masses.

Moreover, there remained the strong Roman respect for inherited forms. Whatever a magistrate or priest might personally believe, he was obliged by his office to perform certain religious rites. But if he performed them as mere gestures without the slightest faith in their efficiency, it was a short step to using them for purely political purposes in the constant struggles and maneuverings for power. The end of the Republic saw an incredibly cynical exploitation of public auspices as a means of obstructing legislation. Needless to say, the masses could not witness such calculated callousness on the part of their leaders without losing their own respect for the institutions.

All roads led to Rome, and they were traveled by thousands of foreigners in the last centuries of the Republic. Slaves, merchants, professional men, and anyone else who hoped to make a living or a fortune in the capital of the Mediterranean world poured into the city. They brought with them their own cults and set up their altars and chapels to serve their religious needs. Romans too who had served as soldiers or administrators in the East or had conducted private business there came home with widened religious horizons.

The earliest foreign cults had been introduced into the city with official sanction—that of Aesculapius, in 293, and that of the Great Mother of the gods, in 205, as ordered by the Sibylline Books. They had been supervised by the state. The former was relatively harmless, since it was concerned with the god's miraculous power of healing. The latter contained repugnant elements, such as eunuch priests and orgiastic dancing and flagellation. No Roman was permitted to take an active part in these rites. When it was discovered that Bacchic rites were being celebrated in Italy by groups of men and women, the Senate intervened vigorously. The cult was not suppressed, but its objectionable features were outlawed, and it was placed under the supervision of the urban praetor. As usual, wild tales had been circulated about the performance of orgiastic rites—the fate of any secret cult, and the Senate was protecting public morals and order. In 139, all "Chaldeans" were ordered to leave Italy. "Chaldean" was a generic name given to a foreign astrologer. The governing class apparently feared the influence on the uneducated masses of the fatalism which they preached.

The first expulsion of the Jews from Rome of which we hear took place in 139. The Jews were very successful proselytizers. To men and women who were bewildered or disgusted by countless gods and goddesses, Judaism offered a welcome monotheism linked to a lofty moral code. The fatal flaw in the eyes of the Roman authorities was the rigid exclusion of all other religious beliefs and practices including those of the traditional Roman religion. The very existence of the gods on whom the Roman state depended for its prosperity and salvation was openly challenged. It was the same uncompromising attitude which led later to the Christian persecutions.

Cults such as those of the Cappadocian goddess Ma, who was identified with the Roman Bellona, and of the Egyptian goddess Isis were brought to Rome unofficially by individuals, and since they did not interfere with public order or the state religion, they were quietly tolerated except when they offended public decorum. The great day of the mystery religions which satisfied man's natural yearning for some certainty beyond the grave by promising their initiates a blissful afterlife had not yet arrived. But the popularity of the cult of Isis showed only too clearly the religious direction which the masses were prepared to follow. The formalities of the traditional religion were cold comfort to many men. The wonderful myth of the sorrow and search of Isis and the resurrection of Osiris gave hope, invited contemplation, and nourished the soul.

It is highly doubtful whether the Augustan religious revival affected the beliefs of the worshiper of Isis, convinced the Epicurean that the gods took some interest in human affairs, substituted in the Stoic's mind a plurality of gods for a single divine providence, gave a faith in divination to the rationalist, made the thief honest, the liar truthful, or the wanton austere. But there can be no doubt that the new and refurbished temples, the sacrifices, the processions and other solemn ceremonies, the increased dignity of the priesthoods, and the whole mighty and splendid apparatus restored and enhanced by Augustus created fresh feelings of respect and awe for the traditional religious institutions of Rome. Those who through habit or belief still clung to the religious ways of their ancestors had their convictions confirmed. Others would be made to think twice before discarding or abusing such hallowed traditions, regardless of their personal attitudes. All Romans could rejoice that the city was as magnificent in her religious life as she was in her wealth, prosperity, and power. All Romans could be content that Rome's relations with the gods had again been set aright.

Although ritual purification was a part of Roman religion, the traditional gods of the city and state were occupied with few aspects of public morality. Marriage, family relations, and the procreation of children were largely matters of custom. The state was interested in the institution of marriage as the source of future citizens and made laws which were designed to protect respectable women and maidens from violation of their persons. But until the Augustan Age, marriage, divorce, and the number of offspring within a family were private affairs with which public authority did not interfere.

We need not examine here the different ways in which a legal marriage could be contracted. But to understand the problems with which Augustus was confronted in the realm of family life, we must recall the legal status of the Roman wife. When a girl married, she either remained under her father's power (*patria potestas*) or passed under the control of her husband in a relationship called *manus*. In the former case she remained economically, so to speak, in her father's family, for her personal property did not come into the possession of her husband and she did not inherit from him. In a marriage with *manus,* her property came to her husband with her person, but she also occupied in the eyes of the law the position of his daughter and had the right to a just share of his estate. Regardless of the status which was chosen, she was equally, in the eyes of the law, the legitimate wife of her husband.

The philosopher Seneca speaks of the time of the Second Punic War (the end of the third century B.C.) as a period in which impurity was a freakish phenomenon, not a vice. He was thinking of course of the chaste behavior of respectable women and girls. Roman society expected the young unmarried man to gratify his sexual appetite and looked with indulgence or amusement on his escapades, provided that his partners in them were women whose honor or reputation he could not tarnish. When he married, society thought it right that he should settle down to the responsibilities of a husband and father. But if he strayed from the path of the faithful husband without seducing another's wife or corrupting a freeborn maiden, the worst penalty which he was likely to suffer was some ugly moments with his outraged spouse, if she got wind of his indiscretion.

The wife's behavior was viewed in quite a different way. She could be promptly divorced for adultery and even instantly killed if caught with her lover *in flagranti delictu.* Fear of being discovered, punished, and disgraced undoubtedly accounted in part for the fidelity of Roman wives during the first three centuries of the Republic. But it was far from being the only motive which assured a wife's correct marital behavior. The Roman family was a tightly-knit unit. The paterfamilias ruled over all his direct descendants while he was alive. His wife was the acknowledged female head of the household. She kept the house in order and raised the children. She mingled with her husband's friends and accompanied him to dinners and other social events. (There were no "women's quarters" in a Roman house.) She was treated with courtesy and deference by all members of her household, and when she went out, the special garment which she wore to indicate her position entitled her to the respect of the passer-by. She participated in the family councils, could appear in court as a witness, had her due place in certain religious ceremonies, such as processions, and although she had no vote and could occupy no official position in Roman political life, she could make her influence felt through the men of her family. A woman thought twice in the old days before running the risk of losing her status as materfamilias.

Moreover, life was fundamentally simple, if not austere, in even the greatest families. Tradition, as embodied in the "ways of the ancestors," was held in high esteem. The performance of duty was a high moral obligation, and one of the most important duties that a man could perform in behalf of his family and his state was to assure the continuing existence of both by marrying and producing children. As the well-being of the state surpassed in importance that of any of its members, so the integrity of the family as a unit took precedence over the personal feelings of its individual members. Adultery in the wife shook the foundations of blood, property, and confidence on which the Roman family rested. It was thus considered just grounds for divorce. Incompatibility was not.

The old standards of marital morality began to fall in the second century B.C. before the wealth which came to the city from the conquests in the East. With the wealth came greed, a taste for the luxuries which had been common in the Hellenistic world, and new, more "sophisticated" ways of acting and thinking. Whereas marriage with *manus* had previously been the most popular form of marriage, women now preferred to remain under the *potestas* of their fathers, especially since the effectiveness of this power was diminishing greatly. Moreover, through a legal device women were enabled to obtain the right to administer their own property when they were not in the *manus* of their husbands. They took advantage of it to become financially independent, and we find married woman with their own financial agents and advisers.

Complete financial independence led naturally to other forms of emancipation in the women of the wealthy classes. The marriages of young girls were arranged by the fathers of the bride and groom, when the latter was in his father's *potestas,* with a view to securing mutual advantages of a political, financial, and social nature. Under the Empire, the consent of both future partners was required for a valid marriage, and it was probably rare in the late Republic that a girl was forced into a union that was repugnant to her. But it was probably equally rare that a sheltered, well-brought-up girl some fifteen years old would oppose her parents' wishes. She was not being married off to fulfill romantic proclivities of her own, if she entertained any, but to be given her due place as a matron and mother in the structure of Roman society.

In instances in which this kind of marriage did not lead to mutual affection or esteem between man and wife, divorce or adultery, or both, were the only paths to a more satisfying physical and emotional union. For centuries, family discipline, the financial and legal dependence of women, a strong sense of duty and decorum, and public opinion had restrained all but a few women from treading these paths. As these obstacles were removed, more and more women turned their feet toward them. Divorces were easily acquired, and although an extra-marital love affair might still bring some unpleasantness in its wake if a husband refused to be complacent, it no longer cost a woman her material wealth or placed her in a position of humiliation, if she had been prudent enough to choose a lover from her own social status.

We naturally hear the most about women of the upper classes whose scandalous behavior attracted the attention of the writers of the period. In all classes there were lasting marriages based on mutual affection, loyalty, and respect. We know of wives who stood heroically by their husbands in the perils of the proscriptions. But the evidence is sufficient to demonstrate that in the upper classes divorce was rapidly increasing with its attendant fragmentation of family relations and that to too many women emancipation meant little more than an opportunity to pursue pleasure and flaunt tradition and custom.

The men of the upper classes were as much, and probably more, to blame for the deterioration of the moral atmosphere. The ruthless pursuit of wealth and power and the placing of personal ambition before the common good naturally undermined standards of conduct in private relations. The gratification of the senses made easily available by power and wealth was more openly pursued. The man no longer had to turn to women of a lower social level, the slave girls, freedwomen, or common prostitutes, to satisfy his sexual appetite. A demimonde had sprung up which offered him companionship, entertainment, and even the illusion of affection on a more cultivated level. And there were women of his own class who were willing to offer him variety in an adulterous affair or to divorce their husbands and enter into a convenient marriage with him.

Under these circumstances the birth rate declined sharply. As early as 131 B.C., the censor Quintus Metellus Macedonicus had proposed that all males be compelled by law to marry for the sake of begetting children. He admitted quite candidly that a wife was a nuisance, but added that she was a necessary one, since the state could not be safe without frequent marriages. To many men, however, the advantages of bachelorhood far outweighed considerations of the public good. As bachelors, they were free of the financial burden of supporting a family and the worries and stresses of married life. The pleasures of connubial relations were easily found outside of the marriage bonds and could be changed and varied at will. A marriage to a rich woman might turn into a nightmare of nagging and humiliation; a marriage to a poor woman had little to recommend it in a society where wealth had become identified with the good life. Finally, the man was surrounded by the adulation, gifts, and subservience of many who hoped to share in his estate. Horace has a biting satire in which he portrays Ulysses asking the advice of the prophet Tiresias in the underworld on the best way to restore his fortune when he returns to Ithaca. Tiresias advises him to become a legacy-hunter (*captator*) and gives him a detailed description of the art. He is to balk at nothing. Even Penelope is to be offered to a rich old childless bachelor, if he takes a fancy to her. The satire, of course, reflects the wide diffusion of the shabby business in Horace's Rome.

In his general program of rehabilitation, Augustus could not ignore the social conditions which we have described above. He had to attempt to make marriage a more desirable and stable condition and the procreation of offspring rewarding. The most important measures were passed in the form of laws in 18–17 B.C. and A.D. 9 which Augustus sponsored and proposed by virtue of his tribunician power.

First, adultery was made the concern of the state by the institution of a public court in which prosecutions for adultery took place. The injured husband had first to divorce his wife formally before witnesses. He was then given sixty days to bring legal action against her. After this period she might be prosecuted in the public interest by any accuser over twenty-five years old. But a husband who was willing to forgive his wife was not compelled to divorce her, and without divorce she could not be prosecuted for adultery. The husband ran the risk of being accused of complicity, but this would be difficult to prove. Augustus wisely let the husband be the first judge of his wife's infidelity. A court could do no more than establish guilt and lay down punishment. The husband had many other things to consider on the human, emotional, and family levels before he decided what action to take.

The court was authorized to inflict punishment on the convicted wife, her lover, and those who had aided them in their illicit relations. Wife and lover were forced to reside on different islands (relegation) for the rest of their lives. The woman was forbidden to remarry a freeborn citizen, and both parties lost a considerable part of their property, the man one-half and the woman one-third together with one-half of her dowry.

The double standard continued to prevail, and a husband, if he prudently refrained from affairs with other men's wives, was in no danger of being prosecuted for adultery. But he could be severely punished for *stuprum,* that is, sexual relations with freeborn maidens and others whose purity the law protected. The prostitute, the kept woman, the unhappy slave girl, he could enjoy with impunity.

The *lex Julia de adulteriis* could not effect any miraculous change in human nature. It did, however, impose a legal procedure for dealing with a moral offense which had hitherto been a purely family affair. It remained a family affair in principle, in so far as the injured husband could decide whether or not to divorce and prosecute his wife for her transgression. But even here the influence of the state's interest must have been felt, because regardless of other considerations the husband knew that if he divorced and prosecuted, he would have to appear in a public role as his wife's chief accuser—and cuckholded husband as well—and that she, if convicted, would suffer a penalty over which he had no control and which he might not desire. This was likely to deter a hasty decision. The penalties which were legally fixed for both partners in an adulterous affair were calculated to make potential transgressors think twice.

Augustus' attempts to raise the birth rate were embodied in the *lex Julia de maritandis ordinibus* of 18 B.C. and the *lex Papia Poppaea,* named after the consuls of A.D. 9. The later law complemented and modified the earlier, and since we do not have the texts themselves, but only references to some of their provisions in later writings, it is often difficult to establish in which law a given article first appeared. It will satisfy our purpose to treat both laws, with certain distinctions, as a single piece of legislation motivated by a basic aim and designed to achieve it through the same general approach.

The basic principle behind the legislation was that citizens, men between the ages of twenty-five and sixty and women between those of twenty and fifty, should marry and produce children. The compulsion consisted in rewards for those who complied with the principle and penalties for those who didn't. A man and woman were completely free to remain unmarried or childless. They would simply have to suffer the consequences of their choice.

Augustus, as usual, was particularly interested in the governing class. Senators and their sons were forbidden to marry freedwomen or freewomen who were engaged in questionable professions. Freemen of other classes were also prevented from marrying the latter, but marriages between freeborn and freed outside the senatorial class were legally valid. The political advantages which came with offspring were limited quite naturally to the senatorial class. The consul who had more children than his colleague was given the privilege of having the fasces during the first month of the consular year. The candidates for the governorship of senatorial provinces did not have to obtain their provinces by lot if they had many children. Presumably, they were given the right to choose where they would go. Men were allowed to stand for public office before the minimum age fixed for each office by law to the extent of one year for each child. This enabled a man to move ahead of his age group, not only at the beginning of his senatorial career at his candidacy for the quaestorship, but, by continuing to increase the number of his children, even further to anticipate the higher magistracies.

Far more effective, probably, were the provisions concerned with financial matters. They were centered around legacies. Blood relatives were not affected, but the law came down heavily on persons outside the family. Unmarried and married but childless persons of both sexes were disabled by the *lex Julia* from taking inheritances or legacies except under the will of a soldier. Marriage and the birth of a child removed this disability. Unmarried women and childless, married women were also subject to a tax on their property. Moreover, widows and divorced women evidently suffered certain disabilities if they did not marry again, regardless of their earlier fertility. The *lex Julia* gave them a year to remarry after the death of their husbands and six months from the time of their divorce. Finally, freewomen who had born three children were emancipated from the necessity of having a legal guardian.

The resistance to the *lex Julia* was probably the strongest which was made to any piece of Augustan legislation. The Romans had a profound respect for a will and a very strong feeling for property. The law deprived the individual of showing his affection or gratitude in the form of legacies to certain persons outside his family after his death. It was also quite unjust in that the unmarried and the married but childless were treated in the same way. Childlessness in married couples could have physical causes over which the partners had no control.

We do not know to what extent the *lex Julia* achieved its purpose within the senatorial class, in which its political rewards were likely to be effective. But we are informed that in A.D. 9, on the occasion of triumphal games held by the consuls to honor Tiberius, the knights urged the repeal of the *lex Julia*. From the speeches delivered by Augustus at the time it is quite clear that the law had failed in this segment of the population. The Emperor scolded, but also faced the fact that some of the harshest aspects of the law had to be mitigated. The changes were embodied in the *lex Papia Poppaea,* of which the most important was the provision that the married but childless forfeited only half of the inheritance and legacies which were left to them. The pecuniary advantages which came to women with three children were also increased.

The Augustan marital legislation long remained on the books. Its principles were considered sound until Christianity placed a new value on celibacy. But the problem which it attempted to solve was by its very nature a private matter in which legal interference was resented and circumvented.

When a society has lost its impulse to expand, artificial stimuli or rewards and penalties rarely produce a thorough or lasting change.

We can fittingly end this chapter by glancing at two of the greatest monuments of the Augustan Age which expressed in concrete form some of the ideas and aspirations which the Emperor attempted to plant in the minds and hearts of the Roman people. Both have been relatively well preserved and occupy conspicuous positions in modern Rome. One has been skillfully reconstructed, and the other has been freed of the accretions of later centuries. They are the Altar of the Augustan Peace, commonly known as the Ara Pacis, and the Forum of Augustus with the Temple of Mars the Avenger which stood in its center.

In the *Res Gestae,* Augustus makes the following statement: "Our ancestors wished the shrine of Janus Quirinus to be closed when peace had been created by victories on land and sea throughout the entire Empire of the Roman people. Although it is recorded that the shrine was closed only twice from the founding of the city to the time of my birth, the Senate decreed that it be closed three times under my principate." The two earlier closings took place in the reign of Rome's second king, Numa Pompilius, and in 235 B.C.; those in the Augustan principate occurred in 29 and 25 B.C. and in a later year which cannot be firmly ascertained but may well have been 13 B.C.

The note of pride in the passage which we have just quoted is not difficult to detect. It implies that the Augustan principate was itself a more peaceful period than all previous Roman history. The people of Rome yearned for peace after the terrible civil and foreign wars which had bloodied the last hundred years of the Republic. Augustus was giving them what they wanted and was impressing the

211

fact on them. The Fourth Book of Horace's *Odes* is filled with praise for the blessings of the Augustan peace. The geographer Strabo states as a simple fact that the Roman people and the provincials never enjoyed such peace and prosperity before Augustus achieved supreme power. If we have interpreted correctly one of the fundamental aspects of the Temple of Apollo on the Palatine, it indicated a new era in which the peaceful arts were to prevail under Augustus' protecting deity.

The Augustan peace, however, did not mean that wars were not being waged by Roman armies to consolidate the frontiers, to pacify tribes within pre-existing provinces, or even to add new territory to the Empire. It is highly probable that Augustus intended to create a new province of Germany which would extend from the Rhine to the Elbe and that his plan was frustrated by the crushing defeat inflicted on the legions by the Germans under Arminius in the Teutoburgerwald. It was even feared at the first report of the disaster that the barbarians might march on Rome and Italy. The fear turned out to be groundless. Even if the Germans had attempted to invade Gaul, there were sufficient troops to turn them back. But in the moments of desperate apprehension, Augustus attempted to raise new troops in Rome. The reaction to this is significant: no one of a military age volunteered for enrollment. The Emperor was compelled to take drastic measures. He selected men forcibly by lot and imposed penalties of confiscation, disenfranchisement, and even death upon the recalcitrant. He called up discharged veterans and broke with tradition by forming units of freedmen.

It is well known that by this time the city of Rome furnished very little of the man power of the Roman army except the higher officers. The Italian municipalities provided the rank and file of the legionary soldiers and the centurions. The noncitizen provincials served in the auxiliary units. But what is striking in the situation which Augustus faced is that the Roman inhabitants of military age could not be moved by an emergency which at first appearance was desperate. It is easy to brush the matter aside with references to degenerate plebs who turned a deaf ear to the appeals of patriotism and duty. But it may also be suggested that the attitude was partly determined by a sincere belief in the unshakable solidity of the Augustan peace which had been inculcated by the Emperor and those who served to propagate his ideas through the arts. Peace did reign in Rome and Italy and to a wide extent in the provinces. A professional army had been organized to do the fighting on the frontiers, and it had usually carried out its missions with success. A people who had been told that peace had come to stay permanently under the Emperor's aegis and who enjoyed its blessings undisturbed could hardly be expected to run to arms at a reversal which must have seemed entirely incompatible with what they saw around them and had been led to believe.

The Ara Pacis was erected by a decree of the Senate as an offering of thanksgiving for Augustus' return to Rome from a successful journey of pacification in Gaul and Spain. The construction of the altar began on July 4, 13 B.C., and its dedication took place on January 30, 9 B.C. It stood on the west side of the Via Flaminia in the Campus Martius at the corner of the present Via del Corso and Via in Lucina. The greater part of the sculptured reliefs were found in the sixteenth century. Additions to them were made through chance discoveries and systematic excavations in the last half of the nineteenth century and the first half of the twentieth. By 1938, sufficient original pieces had been found to justify a complete reconstruction. The altar now stands in the Via di Ripetta between the remains of the Mausoleum of Augustus and the Tiber. The visitor to it should recall that the present orientation is from north to south, whereas its original axis ran from east to west. In describing the monument, we shall refer to the original orientation.

Although the monument as a whole is called an altar, it actually consists of two parts: the altar proper and a rectangular enclosing wall measuring 11.63 meters on the sides with entrances (east and west) and 10.62 meters on the closed sides (north and south). The wall is built entirely of Luna marble and is 6 meters high. The exterior is decorated with two bands of sculpture separated by a meander pattern. The lower one consists of an elaborate floral motif which is repeated at intervals. It is purely and successfully ornamented. Above it are figured scenes on which we must dwell.

The visitor who approached the enclosure from the Via Flaminia on the east saw two panels above the floral decoration, one on each side of the monumental entrance to the altar itself. The panel to the right of the doorway has come down to us in a badly mutilated state. Enough has been preserved, however, for scholars to agree that it contained the allegorical figure of Rome seated on a mass of weapons. The panel to the left of the doorway is well preserved. Its center is occupied by the figure of a seated woman holding two small children. In her lap are fruits, and at her sides are various kinds of plants and flowers. A river flows by her feet near which a cow and a sheep are portrayed on a reduced scale. On each side of the woman in the center is a seated figure framed by a billowing veil. The one on the right is seated on a sea monster, that on the left on a flying swan.

According to the traditional interpretation, the central figure represents Tellus or Terra Mater (Mother Earth). The children, fruits, plants, and animals about her are symbols of her fecundity, and the attendant figures are the fertilizing elements of water and air. This is certainly an attractive explanation. It expresses the idea that the Augustan peace enabled and encouraged the earth to return to her old fertile ways by removing the devastation and destruction with which warfare afflicts all living things.

Yet, we should expect a figure and a scene which afforded a more concrete balance to Rome in the opposite panel. It has therefore been suggested that the figure with which we are concerned represents Italy. This interpretation is less abstract and more convincing.

In the Augustan Age, Italy came into its own as the land which was the core of the Empire. The long process during which Rome had conquered the peninsula and kept some of the Italians in a favored, but politically subordinate, condition had ended. Roman citizenship had been extended from the Alps to the Straits of Messina and was the common citizenship of Italy. All Italians had rallied around Octavian in his struggle with Antonius to preserve the supremacy of Rome, and that supremacy had largely been won by means of the loyalty and fighting ability of Italian men.

In the *Res Gestae,* Augustus emphasizes that a multitude such as Rome had never seen before flowed into the city from all parts of Italy to elect him pontifex maximus. No tax was imposed on Italian land, an exemption denied to provincial land unless it was placed under the "Italian right" (*ius Italicum*). When Augustus divided all Italy in eleven regions, he was not intending to split the country apart. He was rather setting up a uniform system of administration that confirmed the equality of all parts within a unified whole.

215

Rome remained the city from which the Empire was governed. But it was as never before the political capital of Italy. It had long been its literary and cultural center. From the time of Gnaeus Nauvius of Capua (last half of the third century B.C.), Italian writers had come to Rome to seek fame and fortune. This movement reached its peak in the great writers of the Augustan Age. Vergil, from the village of Andes outside of Mantua, Horace, from Venusia on the border of Apulia and Lucania, Livy, from Padua, Propertius, from Assisi, and Ovid, from Sulmo in the Abruzzi, all recalled their birthplaces with nostalgic affection. Vergil and Horace glorified the Roman spirit and Roman tradition. But the Italian contribution to the creation of Rome's greatness was not forgotten, and as in history, so in thought and feeling did Rome and Italy stand together as parts of a large unity. The figure of Italy complementing that of Rome on the panels on the east side of the enclosure was a splendid realization of the Italian idea.

The exterior wall of the enclosure on the west also had a doorway with a panel on each side. The one on the south on the same axis with the Italy panel contains a scene in which the Trojan hero Aeneas is sacrificing a sow on his arrival in Latium in the country near the mouth of the Tiber. The Penates, the household gods which Aeneas brought from Troy to Italy, are shown in a small shrine in the background.

The origin and development of the legend that Aeneas and a band of his fellow Trojans escaped from Troy after it had fallen to the Greeks and emigrated to Italy cannot be analyzed here. It will be sufficient to state that the legend originated in Greek writers and was accepted and modified by the earliest Latin authors. The chief modification was this: There was a Roman tradition which attributed the founding of Rome to Romulus around the middle of the eighth century B.C. But the fall of Troy in the Greek chronology best known to the early Greek writers took place in 1183 B.C. The first Greek authors to write on Rome's foundation either made Aeneas the founder of the city or, having heard vaguely of Romulus as the local founder, left him as such but also made him the son, grandson, or great-grandson of Aeneas. The Roman historians could not accept this close relationship, but wished to keep Romulus in direct descent from Aeneas. Hence they invented a long line of kings who descended from Aeneas and a Latin wife and ruled over Alba Longa until Romulus, their last descendant, founded Rome.

In the last century of the Republic, a number of the great and old Roman families were claiming descendance from the members of the original Trojan migration. The antiquarian Marcus Terentius Varro (116–27 B.C.), the most learned man of his time, even wrote a book on the Trojan families of Rome. Both the Julius Caesars and the Aemilii traced their family lines back to Aeneas himself. But the supreme political power and prestige of Julius Caesar made the direct descent from Aeneas through his son Iulus a family possession. Caesar exploited this pedigree thoroughly. At the beginning of his political career, when he was quaestor (68 B.C.), he stated publicly in a funeral oration which he delivered in honor of his Aunt Julia that his family on his father's side was connected with the immortal gods, since the Julian family descended from Venus (the mother of Aeneas). The splendid temple which Caesar erected in his forum and dedicated to Venus the Mother (of the Julian family) was a monumental assertion of his divine ancestry. We shall see below what use Augustus made of the theme.

Aeneas was also the founder of the Roman race. This

concept was fixed and immortalized by Vergil in the *Aeneid*. There we see Aeneas carrying out the divine mission, against countless hardships, obstacles, and disasters, which will result in the formation of the people whose descendants will found Rome and lead her to the greatness which destiny has reserved for her. The last half of the epic, which Vergil himself considered the more important part of his work, takes place in Latium. It describes the wars which Aeneas had to wage with the native Italic tribes, the Latins in particular, before his conclusive victory opened the path to a peaceful fusion of the Trojans and the native inhabitants. The fusion has a divine sanction, as we learn from majestic speeches of Jupiter and Juno. In customs, language, and name the new people will be Latin. The Trojans will remain as a stratum in its foundation, but the power of the future Roman race will rest on Italian virtue.

Aeneas' sacrifice of the sow in the panel on the Ara Pacis was well known to all readers of the national epic. In the course of his wanderings Aeneas received the prophecy that only when he found a white sow that had recently given birth to thirty young on the bank of a stream would he have found a place to build a city and an end to his wanderings. The prophecy was realized on a bank of the Tiber after Aeneas' arrival in Latium. He sacrificed the animal to Juno.

The Aeneas panel recalled the Italian part of the *Aeneid*. It was a fitting counterpart to the allegorical figure of Italy. Although Aeneas was a Trojan, he was responsible for forging the ancestors of the Roman people out of Trojan and Italian blood, in which the latter was fated to predominate. He himself married an Italian princess and ruled over Italians and Trojans alike. His descendants were kings of Alba Longa, and the last of them founded Rome.

Only a few fragments remain of the panel on the opposite

218

side of the west entrance on the same axis as the figure of Rome on the east side. But it is virtually certain that it depicted Romulus and Remus being suckled by the wolf. Mars, father of the twins, and the shepherd Faustulus, who adopted and raised them, are gazing at the miraculous scene. The salvation of the twins symbolizes the beginning of Rome, and the presence of Mars, the military valor which made Rome great. The panel is an appropriate counterpart to that of the allegorical figure of Rome on the east.

We now come to the north and south sides. On them we find carved two stately processions of men and women. Both move from east to west and represent the individuals who took part in the founding of the Altar on July 4, 13 B.C. All the figures cannot be identified, even when they are completely intact, and the artist seems to have taken some liberties with historical accuracy. But we shall not be far wrong if we describe the procession on the south side as follows.

It is led by the pontifex maximus Lepidus and his attendants. Then, behind a group of lictors, comes Augustus between the consuls of the year, his stepson Tiberius and Quintilius Varus. They are followed by the three major priests of Jupiter, Mars, and Quirinus and the priest of the deified Julius. Agrippa, the Emperor's son-in-law, is at the head of the family group. It includes Livia, Augustus' wife, Julia, his daughter, and one of her sons by Agrippa. Drusus, Augustus' other stepson, and his wife with one of their children, her sister and brother-in-law with two children, and a few of the senior statesmen, such as Maecenas and Valerius Mesalla, who were close friends of the Emperor follow. The procession is headed toward the panel on the west side in which Aeneas makes his sacrifice.

The figures on the north wall cannot be identified by name. But probably they are members of the Senate and

219

the Roman people, two groups which must have been represented at the actual ceremony. They are headed in the same direction as the imperial party, but toward the panel of Romulus and Remus.

The inner walls of the enclosure are also divided horizontally into two registers. The lower register may represent in marble the wooden enclosure which was set up temporarily for the laying of the foundations in 13 B.C. If so, the magnificent festoons of fruits and flowers hanging from ox skulls in the upper register reproduce the original floral decorations. The great altar within the enclosure is also decorated with processional scenes on a smaller scale. In the extant remains we can distinguish the Vestal Virgins and sacrificial animals with their attendants.

The striking thing about the processions on the outer walls is that the artist has caught them at a moment when they are not moving forward. It is clear from the arrangement of the figures on two planes that they are marching in pairs or three abreast. But the halt has had its inevitable effect: groups have stayed together, but any formal order has been broken up. People are chatting with each other, gazing around idly, or lost in their own thoughts. The smaller children clinging to their parents add a delectable note. The adult figures have great dignity in their draped garments. The faces in the figures in the foreground are portraits which are meant to be recognized. There has undoubtedly been some idealization, but the strong Roman feeling for reality and for the work of art as the record of an actual person or event has not been submerged.

If we look at the sculpture of the outer walls from the point of view of history and the mental climate of the period, we are at first impressed by the political relationship of the two processional scenes: the Emperor and his family on one side, the Senate and people on the other. The Emperor has taken a "constitutional" position between the consuls of the year. He is not yet pontifex maximus, so with due deference to religious protocol has allowed Lepidus to lead the procession. The four priests who follow Augustus and the consuls emphasize the sacred character of the event. One of the priests recalls for us that the Emperor is the son of a deified father.

Agrippa stands next in line, not only as the Emperor's son-in-law and the father of two boys whom Augustus has already adopted, but also as the dynastic successor in the event of the Emperor's death. Since 18 B.C. he had shared the Emperor's tribunitian power for a term of five years, and in 13 B.C. the term was renewed. He had been Augustus' chief assistant in the celebration of the secular games and had acted as his viceroy in the East. We should not speak of him as coregent. There was only one Emperor, and everyone knew it. But Agrippa was Augustus' closest political associate at the time, his strong right arm, the father of his grandchildren, and next to him the most powerful man in Rome. Regardless of the forms of the restored Republic, experience had shown that if Augustus was forced to drop the reins, someone with authority and ability would have to gather them up quickly. Agrippa was the man best qualified to do so.

The men, women, and children who follow Agrippa in the foreground are there chiefly because of their relationship to Augustus through blood, marriage, and friendship. But in Tiberius and Drusus, his stepsons, Augustus had younger men who had already distinguished themselves brilliantly in the military service of the Empire and supplied, so to speak, a reserve of dynastic power.

On the other side stood the traditional Republic, exempli-

221

fied in the Senate and the Roman people. We have already examined the role which Augustus assigned to the Senate in his constitution, and we have discussed his attempts to rehabilitate the people as a responsible organ of the government. On the one side, then, was the reality of Augustus' power, carefully veiled by his position between the consuls and his respect for religious forms, but evident in the very fact that he had been able to found a dynasty, and on the other, the long tradition of republican government which was the façade of the restored Republic, and also, in the case of the Senate, an important part of the administrative machinery of the new order.

In the panels on each side of the entrances, Italy and Rome stood forth as elements of equal value in the concept of the motherland and its capital, from which the Empire was ruled. The beginning of each, Roman Italy and the city, were embodied in the legendary heroes, Aeneas and Romulus. Augustus moves toward the founder of his family depicted performing a religious rite such as the one in which Augustus was actually engaged. The Senate and the Roman people approach the man who founded the city, created the first senate, and forged the first population of Rome from Albans, Sabines, and others. This mixture of symbolism and reality, legendary past and historical present, religious piety and dynastic politics, skillfully blended into a work of art of great beauty and profound human interest, is a monumental synthesis of the times.

We have already mentioned that in one of the panels of the Ara Pacis, Mars, the god of war, is watching Romulus and Remus being suckled by a wolf. One of the greatest of the Augustan monuments was erected in honor of this god. A temple to Mars the Avenger was vowed by Augustus on the eve of the battle of Philippi in 42 B.C. It will be recalled that this was the battle in which Augustus took vengeance for his adoptive father's assassination on Brutus and Cassius, the chief conspirators in the plot to kill Caesar. When they had met their deaths, the fulfillment of the vow became a sacred obligation.

Forty years later, on August 1, 2 B.C., Augustus dedicated the completed temple in a new forum of his own construction. In the great apse at the back of the temple stood colossal statues of Mars, Venus, and Julius Caesar. The presence of Mars needs no explanation since the temple was dedicated to him. But he had also long been associated with Venus in myth and was held to be the divine father of Romulus. Of Venus as the divine mother of Aeneas and, hence, the ancestress of the Julian family, we have already spoken. Julius Caesar stood in the temple not only as the father of the Emperor who had avenged his death with filial piety, but also as the founder of the present greatness of the Julian house. The display of his sword reminded the visitor of the brilliant general's own achievements.

Consequently, the temple was in many ways a family memorial. But it was also designed to be a military center where the memory of Roman valor under arms could be preserved and constantly refreshed. It was there that the Senate met to discuss the granting of triumphs. From it officials went forth to their provincial commands and to it they returned, if granted triumphs, to dedicate their crowns and scepters. Military standards recaptured from the enemy were placed in this temple, and young men on reaching the age of military service were urged to make it their particular shrine. Finally, the statues of generals who had celebrated triumphs were erected in bronze in the forum.

The historian Suetonius tells us that next to the immortal gods Augustus venerated the memory of the men who had

223

raised the Roman state from its humble beginnings to a
position of the greatest power. He adds that the Emperor
dedicated statues of all of them in triumphal garb in both
porticoes of his forum. The imperial edict is preserved in
which his purpose in doing so is stated. It was that the lives
of these worthies should serve as a standard by which his
own life and those of his successors should be measured by
the citizens.

In 1925, the Forum of Augustus began to be cleared of
the debris and buildings which later centuries had piled over
it. By virtue of these excavations, we can now understand
precisely what was previously reconstructed rather vaguely
on the basis of literary sources.

Marble bases came to light inscribed with the political
biographies of some of Rome's most illustrious men. First
recorded are the regular magistracies, in descending order
from the consulate to the quaestorship. After them we find
other honors, such as priesthoods, listed chronologically.
Last, outstanding achievements in war and peace are recorded, for example, the subjugation of an enemy people
or the dedication of a temple. Fortunately, provincial towns
such as Pompeii and Arezzo began to follow the example
of the metropolis in honoring the worthies of the past and
were content in some instances simply to copy the inscriptions at Rome. Consequently, the inscribed bases from the
Forum, often in a highly fragmentary condition, can be restored or expanded from material found elsewhere.

Measurement of the remains has shown that the bases
were located in the niches of the two hemicycles that are
still visible today. In each niche stood the statue in marble of
the person to whom the inscription referred. The statues
were of heroic size, and in view of the Roman artist's incomparable skill in realistic portraiture we can assume a striking

resemblance in the features of the head wherever the artist had a trustworthy image from which to work. In the case of heroes of the dim historic past or from legendary times, a type could be reproduced, where one had been developed over the years, or free play given to the imagination. It is now clear that Suetonius confused or threw together the marble statues of the worthies of the past with the bronze statues of the generals who had been accorded triumphal honors after the Forum had been completed. The former stood in the niches of the hemicycles as has been described, whereas the latter were located under the two porticoes, each of which forms a cord across the front of its respective hemicycle.

The names under the marble statues summon forth from the past momentous chapters of Roman history: Marcus Furius Camillus, the capture of Veii; Appius Claudius Caecus, the victory wrung from Pyrrhus of Epirus; Quintus Fabius Maximus, the dark, opening years of the war against Hannibal, and Publius Cornelius Scipio Africanus, its successful termination; Lucius Aemilius Paullus, the conquest of Macedon; Gaius Marius, the defeat of the Germanic hordes; Lucius Cornelius Sulla Felix and Lucius Licinius Lucullus, the war against Mithridates of Pontus and the reconquest of Asia Minor.

It is not only the victories that are mentioned. Rome was too great not to acknowledge her defeats or to recall her terrible periods of civil strife. The sack of Rome by the Gauls (390 B.C.) is mentioned as a simple fact. We are told that Camillus would not allow his discouraged fellow citizens to move in a body to unharmed Veii after the departure of the barbarians. He insisted they rebuild their own city. When a Roman read in the inscription of Marius that he was driven from his country by civil arms and restored to it by the same means, there came to mind one of the bloodiest and most ruthless proscriptions that had ever occurred in Roman history, when the streets literally ran with the blood of Marius' enemies. Yet, some twenty years earlier, Marius had commanded Roman armies that had saved all Italy from devastation by Teutons and Cimbrians and had made a just claim to be called the savior of his country.

The Forum, then, glorified Rome's past through the men who had contributed the most to her greatness. It also honored these men individually in the marble resurrection of their persons and public recognition of their deeds. It was the first Hall of Fame, but in its breadth, position, and purpose it far surpassed anything that has been done since along the same general lines. Situated in the heart of Rome where it would be seen daily by thousands, the Forum of Augustus was a constant reminder of the ability, courage, strength of character, and patriotic devotion which had tenaciously raised a cluster of shepherd huts to the city which dominated the Mediterranean world. There could not be a more effective illustration of the powerful verse of Quintus Ennius, Rome's greatest epic poet before Vergil: *Moribus antiquis res stat Romana virisque* ("Rome stands on her men and ways of old").

The precedent for such collective representation—and precedent weighed heavily with the Roman—can be found in an old custom which was followed in the families of the republican nobility. It will enable us to see new aspects of the Forum.

On the death of a man who had occupied an important magistracy—who had been a consul, for example—a death mask in wax was prepared of the deceased. This image came to rest in a wooden shrine situated in the atrium or great hall of the family dwelling. Over a period of time, a considerable number of such masks would be accumulated by a family that continued to bring forth illustrious sons. Under each shrine an inscription was placed which identified the person and gave an account of his public career. The shrines were arranged with connecting lines in such a way that the spectator could tell at a glance the relationship by blood or adoption of the various persons who were represented. Consequently, there stood in the atrium in conspicuous form a constant and vivid reminder of the family's past greatness as exemplified in its deceased members.

Whatever the origin of this custom may have been, it reflected in historical times some fundamental characteristics of the Roman mind. Looking backward, it expressed veneration for the distinguished men of the past in the only field, public life, in which a Roman of the old Republic could attain true distinction. It emphasized, also, the solidarity of the family, presenting it as a continuing body that changed constantly in its parts yet preserved its integrity as a whole. Looking forward, it encouraged the younger men of the family to emulate their ancestors and to show themselves worthy of a precious tradition into which they had had the good fortune to be born. In truth, they had been born into many privileges, but the atrium stood as a daily reminder that they had been born into as many obligations.

As a taste for lavish decoration began to invade the nobility, more elaborate ways were discovered of honoring the ancestors and of setting forth the family pedigree. In the course of the first century B.C. wax portrait busts were made which were artistically superior to the simple funeral masks and which achieved a more complete representation of the deceased. In some family atria, busts of ancestors leaned out of beautifully embellished shields (*imagines cli-*

227

*peatae*). We also hear of painted representations, the equivalent of our family portraits. The trend reached its natural culmination in full-length statues in bronze or marble.

It can now be seen that the Forum of Augustus was, in spirit, the atrium of a noble house executed on a colossal scale befitting the family to which it belonged. The family was, of course, the family of the Roman people (*gens populi Romani*). The Forum of Augustus presented to this family their greatest ancestors and achievements. The veneration, pride, and spirit of emulation which were aroused in a member of a private family at the sight of the family images and inscriptions in his home would be felt by every Roman who stood in the Forum, regardless of his own immediate lineage. From a national point of view which transcended blood and name, he was a descendant of all the men who had made Rome great.

As we have already seen, Augustus hoped that men would evaluate his life by comparing it with the lives of the men represented in his forum. In other words, he identified himself as their successor in the line of greatness and public service. No one would have questioned his position as the head of the Roman family, and when in the year the Forum was dedicated the Senate, knights, and people bestowed upon him the title "Father of his Country" (*pater patriae*), it was only natural that it was inscribed on a four-horse chariot which was placed in the forum in his honor.

In its reflection of an ancestral custom, its veneration of past glory as an incitement to an even more brilliant future, its martial splendor, and its consecration of the Emperor as the worthy heir of the heroes of the past and the head of the Roman family, the Temple of Mars and the Forum of Augustus teach us a great deal about the way in which Augustus wished his Romans to look at their past, take heart for the present, and see their place and his within it.

# EPILOGUE

OF ALL THE GREAT CITIES of the Western world, Rome alone has given her name to two empires, a civilization, and a universal church. No fact illustrates more clearly the unique position occupied by this city in the history of mankind. Regardless of physical disasters and temporary eclipses, Rome has possessed incomparable greatness throughout her long existence. The governing center of the Roman Empire, the seat of the Papacy, the first city of Christendom, and the capital of a united Italy—these are her titles, and from them power and influence, both material and spiritual, have come and still come to her in stunning abundance.

The genius of innumerable writers has given Rome an existence more lasting than bronze. Because of the fascination which she has exercised on inhabitants and visitors alike, we can see her through the eyes of a Horace or a Goethe, a Juvenal or a Stendhal, to name only a few. We can find her loved, deplored, hated, praised, or cursed. We cannot find her treated with indifference.

The city itself is a vast museum of Western civilization. Within its city limits, we can follow the development of the art of building in an unbroken line from the rude huts on the Palatine to the contemporary masterpiece of the Termini station. A walk through any of the older parts of Rome is a lesson in the changing styles and tastes of centuries. The museums and collections overflow with the remains of pagan

Rome's artistic patrimony. Christian Rome has added to it lavishly. Throughout most of her history, what she could not create herself, she could acquire from others or have created for her. The authority and wealth behind her solicitations have not been easily ignored.

The chain of events which assured Rome of continuing greatness goes back to the Roman Empire. A Roman Empire existed before Augustus, for Rome had already made many of her conquests overseas. But he was the man who at a critical time established the lines along which the Empire was to develop with the city as its center. Three hundred years later, when circumstances demanded a radical reorganization and Rome ceased to be the political capital of the fractured Empire, the work had been done. Rome had achieved her imperial greatness and regardless of her loss in actual power was still recognized as the metropolis of the world which she had created.

By establishing this one world of law and order, in which all men felt themselves to be Romans, Rome did more than bring a few centuries of security and prosperity to many millions of men and women. In the rude West she planted the civilization which is the common heritage of all the countries which are called Latin after Rome's tongue. The cultures of these countries in the course of their development from Roman seeds have enriched and refined the whole Western World. In fact, Western civilization is inconceivable without them.

Nor is Western civilization conceivable without the existence of the Roman church. From the very beginning of Christianity, the Roman Empire made physically possible the rapid propagation of the Christian message. This was realized and admitted by some early Christians who themselves saw in the peace and the security of the Empire an act of divine providence. The Empire provided the incentive and the opportunity for them to organize and centralize the new faith.

As early as the second century A.D., the bishops of Rome were being recognized as the successors to Saint Peter and the heirs of his apostolic primacy. But in addition to this, the very fact that the Roman church was situated in the capital of the Empire gave it a universal character and an authority which the other great Christian communities could not hope to attain. The road was opened which eventually led to the Papacy.

Important as Augustan Rome was as a factor in world history, the city was also interesting in itself. In setting forth its virtues and flaws dispassionately, we are struck, in the light of today's social temper, by the lack of a large, politically responsible middle class, the parasitic nature of the city's economy, and the glaring inequality in the distribution of wealth. But we must recall that many great cities in later times have suffered from the same or similar conditions.

Yet, in Augustan Rome we have watched a great city acquire new beauty, strength, and stability. We have seen it adorned with new monuments, civil and religious, which called upon the Roman to renew his pride in Rome's past achievements and to emulate the proven virtues of his ancestors, to have confidence in himself and his mission of justice and order and peace.

Everywhere we have felt the prudent genius of Augustus at work. His accomplishment should have taught us much about what one great man can do through force and persuasion, rigor and compromise, deed and word, reality and image. He could not turn back time, but he could, and did, place the mark of his greatness in an enduring fashion on the mother city of the Western civilized world.

# SELECTED BIBLIOGRAPHY

ANCIENT SOURCES:

*The Monumentum Ancyranum*. Ed. by E. G. Hardy. Oxford, 1923. The ancient texts and an English translation are also given here, but the comments, with references to other ancient sources, are far more detailed.

*Res Gestae Divi Augusti*. With English translation by Frederick W. Shipley. London and New York, 1924 (in the same volume with Velleius Paterculus, *Compendium of Roman History*). It contains the Latin and Greek texts, an English translation, and brief notes.

GENERAL BACKGROUND:

*The Augustan Empire*. Vol. X in *The Cambridge Ancient History*. Cambridge, 1934. Within the first 606 pages of this book, almost every aspect of the Augustan Age is discussed by various authors. But the emphasis is on political and institutional history.

Frank, Tenney. *A History of Rome*. New York, 1923. Pages 332–415 contain a concise but masterful survey of the Augustan Age.

Hammond, Mason. *The Augustan Principate*. Cambridge, Mass., 1933. A detailed description and evaluation of the Augustan constitution.

Holmes, T. Rice. *The Architect of the Roman Empire,* 2 vols. Oxford, 1928, 1931. A detailed account of Roman history from 44 B.C. to A.D. 14.

Marsh, F. B. *The Founding of the Roman Empire.* Second edition. Oxford, 1927. The first part of this book is concerned with the reasons for the failure of the Republic. The second part describes the historical events between the death of Julius Caesar and the battle of Actium (44–31 B.C.) and the establishment and development of the Augustan constitution.

Shuckburgh, E. S. *Augustus: The Life and Times of the Founder of the Roman Empire.* London, 1905. Although antiquated in several ways, it is still the most satisfactory biography of Augustus in English.


MONUMENTS AND BUILDINGS:

Boëthius, Axel. *The Golden House of Nero: Some Aspects of Roman Architecture.* Ann Arbor, 1960. A brilliant history of Roman architecture. Chapter IV, on the domestic architecture of the imperial age, is particularly pertinent to the physical aspect of Augustan Rome.

Nash, Ernest. *Pictorial Dictionary of Ancient Rome.* London, 1961. The monuments are again listed alphabetically. An up-to-date bibliography follows a brief description of each. There are fine plans and beautiful illustrations of the present remains.

Platner, S. B., and T. Ashby. *A Topographical Dictionary of Ancient Rome.* Oxford, 1929. The monuments are listed alphabetically under their Latin names. Each monument is described with references to the ancient sources and to modern scholarly works in which it is treated. A chronological index at the end allows one to survey the building activities of a given period.

Robathan, D. M. *The Monuments of Ancient Rome*. Rome, 1950. This book surveys all the monuments of the ancient city. But since it is organized by regions or parts, monuments of many different periods are treated in the same proximity in which they actually stood.

ECONOMIC LIFE:

Frank, Tenney. *Rome and Italy of the Empire*. Vol. V in *An Economic Survey of Ancient Rome*. Baltimore, 1940. Chapter I treats the Augustan period. It contains much valuable material on the economic life of the city.

Loane, Helen J. *Industry and Commerce of the City of Rome,* (50 B.C.–A.D. 200). Baltimore, 1938. The most complete discussion of the subject available.

Rostovtzeff, Michael. *The Social and Economic History of the Roman Empire*. Second Edition. 2 vols. Oxford, 1957. Chapter II of this monumental survey discusses the social and economic policies of Augustus at home and abroad.

FREEDMEN:

Duff, A. M. *Freedmen in the Early Roman Empire*. Oxford, 1928. Reprinted with slight changes, New York, 1958. Discusses every aspect of the freedmen's civil, social, and economic position.

RELIGION:

Altheim, Franz. *A History of Roman Religion*. Translated by Harold Mattingly. London, 1938. The section on the Augustan Age emphasizes the part played by the poets

Vergil and Horace in the elaboration of the religious ideas of the period.

Lewis, Martha W. Hoffman. "The Official Priests of Rome under the Julio-Claudians." *Papers and Monographs of the American Academy in Rome,* Vol. XVI (1955). A detailed list of the men who were members of the priesthoods under Augustus and an analysis of the Emperor's policy toward them.

Ryberg, Inez Scott. "Rites of the State Religion in Roman Art." *Memoirs of the American Academy in Rome,* Vol. XXII (1955). Contains important chapters on Augustan religious art, especially the Ara Pacis.

Taylor, Lily Ross. *The Divinity of the Roman Emperor.* Middletown, Conn., 1931. More than half of this excellent book is devoted to the formation and practice of the imperial cult in the Augustan Age.

MISCELLANEOUS:

Carcopino, Jérôme. *Daily Life in Ancient Rome.* Ed. with Bibliography and Notes by Henry T. Rowell. Translated from the French by E. O. Lorimer. New Haven, 1940. Although most of the material is drawn from the post-Augustan Empire, there is a great deal on daily life which is pertinent to the Augustan Age.

# INDEX

# Index

Augustus, Emperor: influence on his period, 8–9; triple triumph, 13; family, 15; Caesar's heir, 16–19; rivalry with Antonius and earliest magistracies, 19–28; member of first triumvirate, 29–31; Philippi, 31–32; Perusine war, 32; treaty of Brundisium, 32–33; war with Sextus Pompeius and Lepidus, 33–36; struggle with Antonius, 40–43; West rallies behind him, 43–44; war against Cleopatra, 45–47; removal of future rivals, 48; special *imperium,* 56; title of Augustus, 56–57; imperial virtues, 57; *princeps* and *auctoritas,* 57–59; title of *imperator,* 59–61; proconsular imperium, 62; rejects dictatorship and consulship for life, 63, 67, 151; rejects censorship, 65–66; "father of his country," 66–67, 228; purges the Senate, 69–70; control of elections, 71–75; genius included in sacrifices, 118–19; house on Palatine, 121; attitude towards dole, 145; recovers standards from Parthians, 153; interest in games, 154; presides over secular games, 156; membership in priestly colleges, 180; pacifies Gaul and Spain, 213; on Ara Pacis, 219; head of the *gens Romana,* 228

Basilica Aemilia: 176
Basilica Julia: 175
Basilica Sempronia: 175
Baths of Agrippa: 101, 126–27
Brutus, Decimus: governor of Cisalpine Gaul, 21; besieged by Antonius, 24; granted triumph, 25
Brutus, Marcus: supported by the Senate, 26; defeat and suicide at Philippi, 31

Caecilius Isidorus: wealth, 142, 148
Caesar, Gaius Julius: great-uncle of Augustus, 14–15; assassination and will, 16–17; relations with Cleopatra, 38, 47; kingly aspirations, 52; month of July named after him, 57; sacrosanctity of tribune, 64; sets legal rate of interest, 142; reorganizes tithes of Asia, 143; number receiving dole reduced, 146–47; creates *aediles Cereales,* 150; new games, 152–53; naumachia, 162; enlarges circus, 163; building program, 173; Forum of, 174; Senate house and rostra, 175; *parens patriae,* 176; temple of, 177; multiple priesthoods, 180; statue in temple of Mars, 223
Caesarion, son of Julius Caesar and Cleopatra: visit to Rome, 37; created king of kings, 40–41; assassination, 48
Campus Martius: in building programs of Caesar and Augustus, 173–74
Cassius, Gaius: supported by the Senate, 26; defeat and suicide at Philippi, 31
Castor and Pollux: temple of, 175
Cato the Censor: builds Rome's first basilica, 123
Catulus, Quintus Lutatius: builds Tabularium, 175

# Index

# ROME

241

THE CENTERS OF CIVILIZATION SERIES, of which this volume is the fifth, is intended to include accounts of the great cities of the world during particular periods of their flowering, from ancient times to the present. The following list is complete as of the date of publication of this volume:

1. Charles Alexander Robinson, Jr. *Athens in the Age of Pericles*.
2. Arthur J. Arberry. *Shiraz*: Persian City of Saints and Poets.
3. Glanville Downey. *Constantinople in the Age of Justinian*.
4. Roger Le Tourneau. *Fez in the Age of the Marinides*.
5. Henry Thompson Rowell. *Rome in the Augustan Age*.